THE TRUSTEE'S ROLE IN
EFFECTIVE ADVOCACY

*Engaging in Citizen Action to
Advance Educational Opportunities
in Your Community*

WHAT TRUSTEES NEED TO KNOW
ABOUT EXERCISING INFLUENCE
ON BEHALF OF COMMUNITY COLLEGES

Published by:

Association of Community College Trustees
1233 20th Street, N.W., Suite 301
Washington, D.C. 20036
www.acct.org
202.775.4667

A Special Project of the ACCT Trust Fund
Library of Congress Catalog Card Number:
ISBN:978-1-886237-00-1

Additional copies of this publication are available for purchase online at www.acct.org

Copies can be ordered by contacting:
ACCT Publications
1233 20th Street, N.W., Suite 301
Washington, D.C. 20036
Printed in the United States of America

ABOUT THE ACCT PUBLICATIONS SERIES

ACCT is issuing this series of publications as part of its new leadership goal to set the standard in education and services by being the nation's foremost publisher of practical resources on board roles and responsibilities for community college trustees. As the only national organization focused exclusively on community college governance, ACCT is committed to providing state-of-the-art guidance, identifying "best practices," monitoring policy and governance issues, and anticipating future community college board needs. Each publication provides an in-depth focus on a topic of importance to boards, offering practical advice, tools, and information on resources available to assist trustees, presidents, and staff.

ACCT's mission is to promote effective board governance through advocacy, education, and services. ACCT addresses the needs of its member boards by identifying and developing board leadership services, offering educational opportunities, sharing information, conducting independent research, issuing publications and related tools, and disseminating leading practices. We are committed to capturing "what works" in community college governance and making it available to our membership and the community at large. We acknowledge the generosity of the ACCT Trust Fund in providing support for the ACCT Publications Series.

Please reach out to us with any questions or suggestions regarding this publication, or to suggest topics of interest to trustees for future publications.

TABLE OF CONTENTS

FOREWORD

Advocacy (n.) – *the act of pleading in favor, or speaking or writing in support, of something*

Community colleges are a tremendous resource to our communities. They employ more than 500,000 individuals, transform the lives of more than 11 million students annually, and on average return $3 for every dollar the public invests directly in a community college.

The citizen volunteers who give of themselves in order to oversee community colleges — community college trustees — are vital to the promotion and well-being of the communities in which they work and live. Whether elected locally or appointed locally or statewide, community college trustees serve as lynchpins, ensuring responsiveness and accountability to the numerous constituencies that have a stake in the productivity and results produced each and every day in the 1,200 community colleges throughout the nation.

This publication is designed to equip community college trustees with the information and insights to prepare and enable them to be successful advocates on behalf of their colleges.

When community college trustees fail to exercise their responsibility to be advocates — to be seen as the face of their colleges in their community — fewer students gain a foothold in the new economy, businesses lose a critical workforce education partner, and community and state economic development suffers.

Being an advocate means taking every opportunity to champion the cause of community colleges by educating policymakers and opinion leaders at all levels about the spirit and transformative power that is today's community college. Trustee advocacy requires passion and drive. But passion must always be informed by data and proven results that compel policymakers to act in the best interests of community colleges and those who depend upon those institutions every day.

Trustees exercise their legitimacy as leaders and advocates by exploiting opportunities to be seen as policy leaders within their communities. They must be honest brokers of information about the needs of their communities and the myriad ways that the colleges they govern affect lives and economies for the better.

When trustees have the ammunition they need to make the arguments necessary to bring about real and positive change, they win the case by getting the public and other stakeholders behind them, and the results can be leveraged. In short, community college trustees help ensure that America remains competitive and a leader in the world economy. It is their avocation; it is their mission.

J. Noah Brown
ACCT President and Chief Executive Officer

ACKNOWLEDGEMENTS

This publication is dedicated to maintaining the tradition established by the thousands of trustees who, since the creation of the community colleges in America, have engaged in citizen action to advance educational and workforce opportunities for their communities. We acknowledge and celebrate the last 50 years of growth and success as community colleges became an integral part of American higher education. As we engage in finding solutions to unforeseen national and global issues, it is imperative for the current and next generations of trustees to exercise their constitutional rights and continue to effectively engage in citizen action on behalf of community college students and the communities they represent. Trustees are the most important part of the federal relations effort for community colleges. This publication serves as a tool for new trustees and new presidents and a refresher for experienced leaders. Section I provides an introduction to and definition of advocacy. Section II covers advocacy at the national level, Section III covers state-level policy efforts, and Section IV addresses effective local-level advocacy. Following these overviews are articles that detail the creation of the U.S. Senate and House of Representatives Community College Caucuses, profiles of two state-based advocacy efforts, and a case study to serve as a tool to encourage discussion. The Appendices are "chock-full" of information on additional resources.

We want to acknowledge the contributions made by the previous ACCT staff in creating the original version of this publication, which was published in 1990, followed by a second edition in 1994. ACCT has been blessed with a dedicated and effective public policy staff including its first Directors of Federal Relations, Frank Mensel followed by Melanie Jackson; former Director of Communications Sally Hutchins; former Legislative Assistant Stephanie Trimarchi Giesecke; current ACCT President and CEO J. Noah Brown; and Jee Hang Lee, ACCT's current Public Policy Director. Sarah Melendez, former Executive Director of Independent Sector, provided valuable assistance, and David Conner, ACCT's Marketing and Communications Specialist, added his magic touch to the final preparations.

This updated publication was inspired by the thousands of citizen trustees and advocates who in the past, present, and future have given, give, and will give freely of their time on behalf of our nation's community colleges. The goals of this book are to offer practical information about how best to advocate for colleges and, through sharing experiences, to capture effective advocacy practices throughout the country. However, the heart and soul of advocacy can only be captured through the collective commitment and involvement of our trustees.

Narcisa A. Polonio, Ed. D.
Vice President
Education, Research, and Board Services

INTRODUCTION

Active, effective trustees working in partnership with their presidents or chancellors at local, state, and national levels have made a significant difference in the pursuit of policies that provide the resources and environment for community colleges to best serve their students and communities. They have helped build a national network of community colleges that today enroll 11.7 million students — close to half of the undergraduate students in the United States. Community and technical colleges can be found within commuting distance of almost every town, city, or community in every region of the country. They provide educational opportunities for all who desire to avail themselves of the opportunity to attend a transfer or career program, workforce training, or life-long learning opportunities. Community colleges are integral to the economic well-being of local communities throughout the nation. As America's unique contribution to higher education, community colleges reflect our democratic principles of inclusiveness and opportunities regardless of background, heritage, or economic status. These principles are also reflected in the governance structure made up of more than 6,000 citizen trustees who freely give of their time to serve.

Trustees are responsible for setting the policies for community colleges on whose boards they serve. But they have a second, equally and sometimes even more important responsibility: they must be active, effective advocates for not only their own community colleges, but also the more than 1,177 community and technical colleges around the country and the students and communities they serve. Trustees' advocacy is essential to the pursuit of national, state, and local policies that benefit the colleges they represent, and to the opposition to policies that would hurt them.

This publication is intended to help trustees become effective players in the policymaking and legislative processes by providing some time-tested ideas, strategies, and tactics for exercising their voices and influence on behalf of the their colleges, students, and communities at the highest levels of policymaking in the nation's capital. It is intended to be a basic primer and to provide advice and hints for working with federal lawmakers. These same techniques can also be applied to state and local advocacy efforts.

This publication updates the original ACCT *Effective Advocacy*, published in February 1994. This update is divided into sections in order to best serve the various needs of readers. Some information is repeated among the federal and state-specific sections; however, this information is nuanced and tailored to the needs of each specific area. We encourage you to read through each section, in order to best understand the complexities of advocating for community colleges at the local, state, and federal levels.

Section I of this text serves as an introduction to community college advocacy. Section II covers advocacy at the national level, including a section on how national policy priorities are defined and pursued by community colleges, a brief overview of the basics on the legislative policy process, and some ideas and strategies to increase your effectiveness.

Section III covers state-level policy efforts, and Section IV addresses effective local-level advocacy. Following these overviews are articles that detail the creation of the U.S. Senate and House of Representatives Community College Caucuses, future steps for community college advocacy, and profiles of state-based advocacy efforts. The appendices provide resources that will help you make sure your voice is heard by your legislators.

Members of Congress, state legislators, and local representatives share their constituencies with community college trustees, making all parties natural allies in pursuit of policies to benefit their constituents.

Effective Advocacy by Community College Trustees: The Fundamentals

EFFECTIVE ADVOCACY

Trustees, in partnership with presidents, have both the opportunity and the responsibility to take an active role in shaping public policies that benefit the communities served by the colleges they govern. Trustee advocacy adds credibility and leverage to policymaking efforts at the national level. Engaged trustees, working together, can and do make a difference for their communities each and every day, both by representing the voices of the communities and by adding grassroots participation locally, in state capitals, and in the nation's capital, Washington, D.C.

While elected officials at all levels have the responsibility to allocate tax dollars to fund community colleges, they must also provide funding for many competing — and often deserving — public services. In a democratic society, **all groups have an equal right to influence the decisions made by their elected officials** and thus, the distribution of tax dollars. The commonly held negative views of lobbyists and their alleged abuses of influence sometimes obscure the positive aspects and resulting benefits to society of advocates. There is a big difference between a paid lobbyist (someone who is hired to influence) and citizen who takes action. Trustees are elected or appointed to serve their colleges and communities as public officials dedicated to serve the public good, which lends credibility to their advocacy efforts. They are seen as altruistic and not self-serving in their efforts on behalf of community colleges. The relationship deepens at the state and local levels, as many trustees are appointed by state legislatures or governors, or directly elected by local voters. This direct link to the public and to elected officials can be a valuable connection, as can the relationship between the community college president and trustees. Constituents who advocate for a cause, either individually or in groups, **are engaging in citizen action to help their legislators and elected officials to be more responsive to their needs. Trustees engage in citizen action on behalf of the greater good of our society and as part of their responsibility to ensure funding for community colleges.**

Members of Congress, state legislators, and local representatives share their constituencies with community college trustees, making all parties natural allies in pursuit of policies to benefit their constituents. Elected officials rely on their constituencies to help them understand the needs of the people and institutions they represent and how best to serve them. Community college trustees are in an excellent position, from a grassroots and campus perspective, to both speak up and provide policy guidance to legislators on behalf of community colleges.

The president articulates the facts and needs and provides the vision, and trustees bring the passion as members of the community. Thus, healthy and active partnerships between college trustees and presidents are vitally important for advocacy at the state and national levels.

WHAT IS ADVOCACY?

Advocacy describes all of the activities undertaken by a particular group or individual to influence the actions of local, state, and national lawmakers. These activities range from letter writing to full-scale lobbying. Much local and state advocacy is done on a "grassroots" level by those who live in the community and have a vested interest in it. ACCT is the trustees' voice in Washington, D.C., advocating on their behalf at the national level. For boards and trustees, advocacy can take many forms, including building relationships with elected officials at the national, state, and local levels, preparing position papers, seeking sponsors for legislation, involving faculty, students, and other groups, sponsoring or hosting public hearings, and creating partnerships with other influential organizations. The merits of each of these forms will be elaborated upon in this book.

WHEN IS ADVOCACY APPROPRIATE?

It is the responsibility of the board as a group and individual trustees in partnership with their presidents to apply their influence to the betterment and protection of the community college. Advocacy is an appropriate vehicle for bringing pressure on elected and government officials for the greater good of the community. Advocacy is an important part of the job description for the board, trustees, and the president.

WHAT ARE SOME BASIC ELEMENTS OF EFFECTIVE TRUSTEE ADVOCACY?

To advocate effectively for their community college, the board of trustees should:

» **Learn the basics of the legislative process** (See pp. 20) and the appropriate terminology (See glossary of terms, Appendix A).

» **Build a relationship** with Senators and Representatives before asking them for support. This will increase the chances of a prompt response to a call or letter in the future.

» **Invite legislators** to visit the campus. If time permits, include a tour of the campus, and plan for the visitors to meet some students.

» **Know the issues.** Obtain a copy of the current statement on community college priorities from ACCT. (Contact ACCT's public policy department at 202-775-4667 or publicpolicy@acct.org.) Know how the issues affect the college and students, the community, and the state and city. The college's public policy staff and ACCT's public policy department can provide information.

» **Attend the ACCT National Legislative Summit** held every February in Washington, D.C.

» **While in Washington, D.C.,** visit senators and representatives on Capitol Hill and urge support for community college priorities.

» **Respond promptly to "action alerts"** issued by ACCT public policy staff. Regular participation in advocacy efforts will ensure that the college and its board will remain on your legislators' radar.

» **Send copies of any letters and e-mail messages** to the ACCT public policy staff.

» **Support and encourage** the president's role as an influential advocate at the state and local level.

» **Understand the connectivity** of the role and level of financial and programmatic support provided to the college from federal, state, and local sources.

WHAT IS THE ROLE OF THE BOARD?

It is part of the board's responsibility, in partnership with the president, to establish legislative priorities and to take necessary actions when appropriate. The board that **"speaks with one voice"** builds credibility and is more effective. The most effective boards "speak with one voice" by identifying common goals and talking points — and supporting the president's effort to build relationships with key legislators, the governor, and other government officials. The board has the means to influence and mobilize the involvement of faculty, staff, and students on behalf of the college.

Presidents and boards develop legislative priorities or/and an advocacy action plan. The advocacy action plan should correlate to current sources of support and the potential for additional and new sources of support. Part of this responsibility is having a clear understanding of the level of funding and resources the college receives from federal, state, and local government. For example, what percentage of the college's operation is being supported by federal grants? What proportion of tuition funded through federal or state financial aid is awarded directly to students? This type of analysis and information helps focus on how best to acknowledge the support being provided and to protect and ensure continued support from the government.

Advocacy is not just about funding. It also involves the many regulations and guidelines established by government and the impact on the college. For example, reporting requirements and oversight can have a significant impact on the college.

Effective advocacy on behalf of community colleges must influence decision making at all three levels of government:

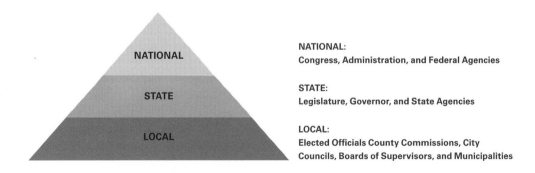

NATIONAL:
Congress, Administration, and Federal Agencies

STATE:
Legislature, Governor, and State Agencies

LOCAL:
Elected Officials County Commissions, City Councils, Boards of Supervisors, and Municipalities

FEDERAL FUNDS WORKSHEET: IMPACT OF FEDERAL EDUCATION DOLLARS ON YOUR CAMPUS

When completed, this form will demonstrate how federal student aid funds and other federal funds are currently at work on your campus. Members of Congress, state legislators, local government officials, and members of the press find this information valuable as they analyze the impact of the many policy changes currently being considered by Congress. Contact your college's student financial aid or business office to assist you in completing this form.

Even if you are unable to complete all the categories listed on this form, Members of Congress and their staffs will find any information you are able to provide them useful when considering the impact of program funding on their districts.

Name of college: _____

FEDERAL PELL GRANT SUMMARY

Award Year	Number of Recipients	Average grant per student	Total grant dollars disbursed
		$	$
		$	$
		$	$

OTHER FEDERAL PROGRAMS

	Fiscal Year	In Dollars
Number of State Scholarship awards made with Federal Leveraging Educational Assistance Partnerships (LEAP) match		$
Total State Scholarship funds awarded with LEAP		$
Number of Federal Supplemental Educational Opportunity Grant (SEOG) recipients		$
Federal SEOG funds awarded		$
Number of Federal Work-Study program workers		$
Federal Work-Study program funds awarded		$
Number of Federal Direct and/or FFELP loan recipients		$
Average loan amount per recipient		$
Total Federal Direct and/or FFELP loan funds disbursed (subsidized and unsubsidized)		$
Number of Federal Perkins loan recipients (if applicable)		$
Community Based Job Training Grants (CBJTG)		$
TRIO funds (if applicable)		$
Perkins Career and Technical Education Act funds in current budget		$
Title III-A (Strengthening Institutions) Grants funds (if applicable)		$
Title V (Hispanic-Serving Institutions) Grants funds (if applicable)		$
Other Federal Programs (list) no room for a. b. c.		$
Summary of Federal dollars assisting students and the institution (sum of lines 2, 4, 6, 9, 12, 13, 14, 15, and 16)		$

Source: The Federal Funds Worksheet was developed by ACCT a tool for use at the annual National Community College Legislative Summit.

CASE STUDY
The Ethics of Advocacy

by Narcisa A. Polonio

PART 1: THE AMBITIOUS BOARD CHAIR

Jane was enjoying the drive home from the board meeting. She smiled at the thought of sharing the news with her family — the news that, after having served as a board member for three years, she had been selected as the new chair of the New Horizons Board of Trustees.

This was her opportunity to shine and gain state-wide visibility. She hoped her term as chair would be the first step to a more prominent appointment by the governor. All of her brothers held prominent positions in the state and her older brother served in the state university board of regents. She knew her father would be proud.

The New Horizons Board of Trustees is responsible for governing and setting policy for the state's 15 community colleges, and appointing the chancellor for the system and the president for each of its colleges. The governor appoints all of the members of the board for five-year terms.

Jane enjoyed serving on the board and believed she had paid her dues in the last three years by learning about community colleges and the role and responsibilities of the board while waiting patiently for her opportunity to take the helm.

Jane felt that the board members took a back seat to the chancellor of the system. In her opinion, the chancellor did not utilize the political expertise of the trustees, nor did he leverage their influence in the statehouse. She felt that the board members should assume a more active role in advocating for the community college system. Many of the trustees had personal relationships with the governor and many other state legislators. They were in a better position to represent the interests of the community college system. After all, the chancellor and presidents were employees and the trustees had greater ties to the community and longstanding relationships with key leaders in the state.

Jane also believed that the administration was not as vigilant as it should be in both watching and responding to legislation that would be in the best interest of community college students. At the state level, there was more attention and focus on the needs of K-12 and the universities and very little attention given to the community colleges. During family gatherings, Jane's brother was always seemed to be bragging about how well the state university was supported by the legislature. Jane took every opportunity to explain that over

40 percent of the state's higher-education students were enrolled in a community college, and yet community colleges only received 15 percent of the higher-education budget. This was an unfair distribution of resources, as Jane saw it.

Looking toward the future, the community college system was facing some difficult financial decisions, as it would have to compete for limited state dollars in the coming years. In Jane's mind, it was crucial to position the state's community college system as a critical player in the future economic vitality of the state. It was time for community colleges to receive the recognition they deserved and, more importantly, they needed more financial support.

Jane believed that her connection to the new governor would be helpful. Her entire family had actively supported the governor's campaign and made significant contributions. Her father had served in the House of Delegates for more than 20 years and still had strong ties with many legislators. He could be instrumental in helping her arrange meetings with key elected officials.

As Jane pulled her car into her driveway, she made up her mind to get moving as soon as possible to set up appointments with key elected officials. She could easily organize a social event at her house and host many of the key political leaders of the state. As a matter of fact, the governor's birthday was coming up, and hosting a party to celebrate the occasion would be a great first step to gain greater visibility for the board and the college. Jane quickly made a mental list of key people to call in the morning to get things organized. She decided to send an e-mail first thing in the morning to invite all of the other board members to the party. She was determined to protect the interests of the community colleges and to start her tenure as chair of the board with a big celebration.

QUESTIONS FOR DISCUSSION

» Is Jane on the right track in attempting to move the state board into a more proactive and influential position with state government? On what grounds is your answer based?

» What are the implications for the board?

» What are the implications for the chancellor, who usually deals with state government officials on behalf of the board and the system?

» Jane's mental to-do list included the following. What aspects of this list are appropriate and which aspects may be considered inappropriate given Jane's role as a trustee and incoming board member?

» Contacting the governor's wife, to obtain her input on an appropriate birthday gift for the governor

» Contacting Jane's secretary, who would compile and send out the invitations as soon as a date was selected

» Reaching out to the catering company owned by her sister-in-law to prepare a menu for her review

» Requesting that the chancellor set aside around $20,000 to pay for expenses, which may include food, entertainment, and beer, wine, and champagne to toast the governor.

STOP.

Before going further, take a few minutes to think about why you answered the questions above the way you did. Are all of the correct answers clear, or could the answers change depending on variable circumstances? What circumstances might change the appropriateness of Jane's actions? (For example, if she personally raised the funds for her welcome party, would this change whether it is appropriate or not? What if she paid out of pocket? Would not throwing a birthday party be considered a missed opportunity for Jane and her fellow trustees to advocate for the college? If Jane has questions about the ethical implications of her ideas, with whom should she discuss her concerns — the board, the chancellor, her secretary, her husband?)

Discuss these and other questions you may have before proceeding to the next section.

PART 2: THE APPROPRIATE ROLES OF ADVOCATES AND ADVOCACY

The Appropriate Role of the Chair
» The chair of the board is one among equals, responsible for helping facilitate the work of the board. The board chair's first interest should be to help the college.
» Being an effective chair requires building trust, team building, being inclusive, and demonstrating respect.
» The chair sets an example and establishes the standards of conduct during the board meetings.
» The chair should seek advice from other trustees, the chancellor and legal counsel with whom discussing privileged information is appropriate before making unilateral decisions that will affect the college financially. Just as an effective board speaks with one voice, it should also agree before taking any major action that will affect the college or its standing.

The Board/CEO Relationship
» It is important for the chair and the rest of the board to respect and support the administration and, in turn, it is important for the administration to request and keep the board informed.
» The board/CEO partnership is based on creating a spirit of cooperation and mutual support and understanding the difference between policy and administration.

Effective Advocacy
» To effectively advocate on behalf of students and community colleges requires a coordinated effort to include different constituencies and key stakeholders, including faculty, students, staff, community members, and other involved parties. Celebrations, social gatherings and parties serve an important role; however, they are only one small aspect of an effective advocacy strategy. Effective advocacy requires planning, the establishment of clear priorities, and the involvement of many constituencies. All advocacy activities should serve a common purpose that has been

agreed upon by the full board and chancellor.

» Effective advocacy is based on building relationships based on respect, mutual interest, and commitment to students, not the self-interests of any board member, whether it is the chair or another trustee.

Avoiding Conflicts of Interest and Upholding a Code of Ethics

» The role of the board and individual trustees is to represent the greater good and serve the community. It is a public trust and should not be used for personal gains.

» The good intentions of an individual can be easily overshadowed by the perception of personal gain or self-promotion.

» Any trustee, including the chair, who has questions about the ethical appropriateness of any action should seek advice from the board's legal counsel.

» The board should adopt a code of ethics and avoid any perception of personal gain and conflict of interest.

Narcisa A. Polonio, Ed.D. is vice president for research, education and board leadership services for the Association of Community College Trustees.

Your Eyes and Ears in The Nation's Capital: Defining and Promoting National Community College Policy Priorities

The Association of Community College Trustees (ACCT) cooperates with its sister organization, the American Association of Community Colleges (AACC), in developing, articulating, and pursuing common national community college legislative priorities. By working cooperatively, the two associations are able to create and pursue a unified voice in support of communities across the nation.

Trustees are the most important contributors to the federal relations effort for community colleges nationally. ACCT and AACC lead national advocacy efforts on behalf of community colleges through the annual Community College National Legislative Summit (NLS), the development of the U.S. Senate and House of Representatives Community College Caucuses, and through related activities that take place primarily in Washington, D.C. ACCT and AACC work closely with their respective members on a "grassroots" level to identify areas of priority concern emanating from communities, states and regions that constitute our memberships.

ADVOCACY AT THE NATIONAL LEVEL

ACCT offers many resources to assist boards and trustees with advocacy at the national level. Among these are:

» The annual Community College National Legislative Summit in Washington, D.C.
» Provide summaries of key legislation and positions taken by Members of Congress regarding key legislation
» The Legislative Action Center at www.acct.org, which offers public policy updates and other resources, including direct links to connect community college leaders with their representatives on Capitol Hill.
» Latest Action in Washington (LAW) E-Alerts — Updates on legislative actions that affect community colleges, e-mailed to subscribers as they happen. To subscribe, e-mail publicpolicy@acct.org with "LAW E-Alert" in the subject line.
» AACC/ACCT Joint Legislative Agenda. Using the Joint Legislative Agenda to develop talking points and action items helps deliver a clear, unified message to legislators, which yields better results than disparate messages.

» U.S. Senate and House of Representatives Community College Caucuses. These Caucuses develop and nurture relationships with advocates within the U.S. Congress and clearly identify community colleges as a national priority.

» ACCT publications, including *Trustee Quarterly* magazine and the *From the Desk of ACCT* newsletter, which offer important legislative updates from around the nation.

» Local visits to congressional representatives. ACCT offers resources to help organize your visit and your message in order to yield the greatest possible results. Contact publicpolicy@acct.org for more information.

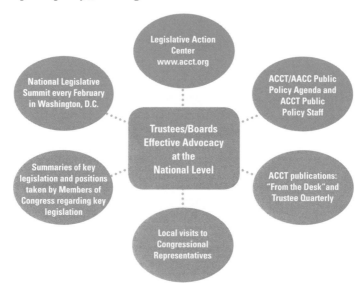

HOW ACCT DEVELOPS A POLICY AGENDA

Through collaborations with other national leaders and ACCT members, as detailed above, ACCT staff uses a variety of venues and communication tools to advocate on behalf of community colleges. These efforts include conducting periodic surveys and interviews to solicit input and perspective from trustees and presidents on federal priorities and needed initiatives. With the assistance of the ACCT Public Policy Committee and AACC/ACCT Joint Commission on Federal Relations, State Association Executives, and State Boards, priorities are reviewed and refined, and then brought forward to the ACCT Board of Directors for endorsement and addition to the association's public policy agenda and goals. AACC follows a similar process involving presidents and chancellors.

THE ACCT/AACC JOINT COMMISSION ON FEDERAL RELATIONS

The Joint Commission on Federal Relations is a deliberative body that assists both ACCT and AACC in focusing on a proactive, future-oriented federal relations agenda. The agenda embodies a strategic vision that serves to promote and advance federal legislation that supports the mission of community colleges in providing education, workforce development, and economic development on behalf of their communities.

The Commission's goal is to help ensure that both associations take public policy positions that are in accord with their respective memberships and that promote unity in their advocacy efforts.

The Commission is charged with:

» Assisting each association board by identifying and gathering information on future trends and important issues;

» Recommending positions to facilitate the setting of a proactive federal relations agenda supporting the broader public policy objectives of each association;

» Focusing both memberships and staffs on the common agenda; and

» Monitoring progress toward achieving shared agenda priorities.

When they consider what action to take on a bill or an allocation,
Members of Congress think about who is asking for their support, their
own personal feelings, convictions, and values, the good of their
constituents, the good of the country, political reality
(is it worth using political capital?), and whether
it will help them get re-elected.

Proposed policies and priority concerns solicited by both ACCT and AACC are submitted to the ACCT/AACC Joint Commission on Federal Relations for consideration and recommendation. The Joint Commission is comprised of eight trustees from ACCT and eight presidents from AACC. Five trustees serving on the Joint Commission are members of the ACCT Board of Directors, with the remaining three trustees coming from ACCT's membership. At least five of the presidents serving on the Joint Commission are AACC Board of Directors members. The ACCT/AACC Joint Commission on Federal Relations carefully considers the issues and recommended policies and then makes a recommendation on a joint policy agenda to the two association boards for action.

ACCT and AACC Board Role

The ACCT Board and the AACC Board each review the recommended agenda, make additions or revisions, and then approve the joint agenda. Once approved by both boards, the community college agenda has the strength of both associations standing behind it, at which time it is forwarded to all Members of Congress and the administration as the policy priorities of community colleges and the communities they serve.

Communicating Policy Priorities

At the outset of each new Congress, the community college agenda statement is published jointly by ACCT and AACC and distributed to all Members of Congress. The Joint Legislative Agenda serves as the community college institution's recommendations to Congress and the administration. The Joint Agenda also is used to guide the membership and association staff in their liaison work. It can also be used to develop talking points or as a reference guide for trustees in their letters to or visits with Members of Congress. The current agenda statement is available from ACCT's Department of Public Policy and available through ACCT's Web site, www.acct.org.

Your Washington Staff

By joining forces, the public policy staff at ACCT and AACC maximize the effectiveness of their efforts on behalf of community college leaders. ACCT policy staff coordinate ACCT and trustee efforts on behalf of community college leaders, and convey an omnipresent image of "one voice, one agenda" for community colleges in Washington. ACCT staff maintains daily contact with Members of Congress and their staffs to advance community college priorities. The staff also seeks to secure opportunities for community college trustees to make their voices heard on behalf of the communities they serve, and to keep ACCT at the forefront of major policy activities in the nation's capital.

ACCT's policy staff keeps trustees informed on the status of priorities through the ACCT Web site — specifically the Advocacy section, which includes Latest Action in Washington E-Alerts — as well as through the ACCT magazine *Trustee Quarterly;* the *From the Desk of ACCT* newsletter; periodic legislative and action alerts through the Legislative Action Center as developments warrant; and through presentations at state association meetings, the ACCT Annual Community College Leadership Congress, the AACC Annual Convention, and the Community College National Legislative Summit.

When developments warrant or when time is of the essence, ACCT staff issues "call to action" alerts that urge trustees and presidents to write, e-mail or call their Members of Congress about a specific and timely issue. Most of the time, such contacts can be made with one or two mouse clicks through ACCT's Policy Center, a Web-based communications tool available to every trustee through the ACCT Web site. By responding to such calls to action, trustees provide the local link that frequently makes the difference in the success or failure of community college-related legislation. The importance of trustees making direct contact with peer-elected officials from their communities can never be overstated.

The ACCT public policy staff is available to answer questions and to assist trustees in becoming effective advocates on behalf of community college priorities to Congress. Contact ACCT staff members at 202-775-4667 or toll-free at 1-866-895-ACCT (2228). You may also e-mail publicpolicy@acct.org.

CARRYING THE COMMUNITY COLLEGE MESSAGE TO CAPITOL HILL: THE COMMUNITY COLLEGE NATIONAL LEGISLATIVE SUMMIT

Coinciding with start of every new Congressional session, ACCT, with the support of AACC, convenes the Community College National Legislative Summit (NLS) in Washington, D.C., each February. NLS is an unparalleled and unique event that provides the latest information and is designed to advance understanding of the issues before Congress and the administration that affect community colleges. The NLS is designed to facilitate opportunities for trustees to "carry the community college message to Capitol Hill." The focal point of community college federal advocacy efforts, NLS draws up to 1,100 community college trustees and presidents from all across the country for three days of intensive interaction with federal policymakers, political experts, and peer stakeholder organizations around the community college policy agenda.

The Summit does more to move community college priorities forward in a Congressional session than any other single event because of the sheer number of trustees who attend, become informed on the issues, and actively participate in the community college advocacy effort. Federal policymakers look forward to seeing their trustees annually, and relationships are advanced year-round.

PREPARING FOR THE MEETING WITH MEMBERS OF CONGRESS DURING THE NATIONAL LEGISLATIVE SUMMIT

Face-to-face meetings are still the best way to communicate the community college message to Members of Congress. With good planning and preparation, meetings can be very productive. In many states, the state association will take the lead in organizing meetings with Congressional representatives.

There are some basic guidelines to keep in mind when planning a visit:

» **Schedule your appointment** well in advance. Keep yourself as flexible as possible. Members of Congress often need to juggle appointments at a moment's notice. You may need to meet with your legislator in a hearing room, a cafeteria, the hall, or the House or Senate lobby. (The term "lobbyist" originated from the last setting.)

» **Involve as many trustees** and presidents from different colleges in your state and region as possible. It may be easier to obtain an appointment as a group than as individuals. Legislators are also less likely to skip an appointment with a group.

» **Make the appointment,** call 202-224-3121 (the Capitol switchboard) and ask for the office of your Representative or Senator, then for his or her appointment secretary or scheduler. Give your name and that of your community college, your city, and the issue you wish to discuss. Inform the scheduler of the size of the group.

» **Prepare for the visit** by becoming familiar with the legislation or issue you will discuss in your meeting. Use fact sheets, issue briefs, or other information provided by the ACCT Public Policy staff or the ACCT Web site for information and guidance about the goals of the legislation. If possible, read the actual bill and be prepared to discuss specific points.

» **Take along, if possible, a community/business leader** who is expert on the issue. If possible, also bring a student or two.

» **If you plan to visit more than one legislator, allow sufficient time** to allow for possible delays and to permit you to get to the next appointment on time.

» **Be on time** and willing to wait.

» **If your appointment is delayed, use the time to get to know the staffer.** Remember that the staffers do the actual work of research, writing bills, and managing your Senator or Representative's schedule and priorities. Staffers can be good allies.

» **Plan to listen.** The Member of Congress may have prepared remarks. He or she may see this as an opportunity to provide an overview of his or her own work efforts and priorities.

» **Pick a spokesperson** in advance. Agree on the key points of the presentation. You may want to give each member of the group an assignment to speak to one point. The member of the group who knows the legislator best, or the one who set up the appointment, should start the discussion.

» **Be clear about who you are,** what college you represent, and what you want. The Member of Congress or staffers should leave the meeting with a good understanding of the importance of the bill or issue under discussion as it relates to community colleges and their students and communities.

» **Keep it simple.** Plan your presentation to last, ideally, five minutes and no longer than ten. Begin by thanking the Member of Congress or staff person for allowing you the opportunity to meet with him or her. Ask for favorable consideration of your position, but understand that the Member of Congress or staff person may not be in a position to make a firm commitment on the spot. He or she may make a commitment to do the best he or she can. The most likely response would be an agreement to consider the proposal.

» **Thank him or her for past support** for the community college agenda or that of your particular college.

» While you may be very experienced at advocacy, it helps to have a **"dress rehearsal"** with a group. This reduces the possibility of going off message and rambling. This also helps keep you within the planned time limits.

» **Take handouts** with you to leave with the Member of Congress or staffer, such as a brochure of your college and a fact sheet (no more than one page each) about the potential impact of the legislation on your college.

» **Be prepared to answer questions.** The Member of Congress will likely ask you questions about the issue and your college. You may want to brainstorm with your group about possible questions so that you are prepared to answer confidently. If you do not know the answer, promise to find out and get back to the Member of Congress or staffer, and then do so promptly.

» **Listen carefully.** The Member of Congress or staffer may have important concerns about the issue, or some suggestions that might help you in promoting your position. He or she may know of colleagues with an interest in the issue or bill and may be willing to circulate a "Dear Colleague" letter, speak with other Members, or send a letter detailing your request to the chair of the relevant committee. **Make notes on all comments and suggestions and forward them to the ACCT Public Policy staff.**

» **Keep the visit positive, friendly, informal, and brief.** Stick to the issue and the facts. Do not be put off by an apparent lack of interest or skeptical reaction. Do not be defensive or confrontational. Never make threats. Do not burn bridges by insulting or ignoring a staffer, no matter how insignificant his or her role may appear to be. Do not make disrespectful remarks about the current administration or any Member of Congress.

» This is a great opportunity to **take photographs** with your representatives. Designate someone to coordinate and take pictures.

» Do not speak negatively or with disrespect about a Member of Congress or staffer while you are still in the building. **You never know who may be listening.**

» As soon as you return home, **send a thank you letter,** spelling out any areas of agreement that you may have reached during the visit. Discuss your future plans on the issue, if appropriate. Ask to be kept informed of Congressional action on the issue.

» Have your college's public relations officer **issue a press release** on the visit to the local media.

» **Keep ACCT informed.** Send an e-mail message about your visit and the exchange to the ACCT Public Policy staff. They will be able to use the information in follow-up contacts. E-mail publicpolicy@acct.org.

THE BASICS OF THE LEGISLATIVE PROCESS

Only Members of Congress can introduce legislation and, by doing so, they become the sponsor(s). There are four basic types of legislation: bills, joint resolutions, concurrent resolutions, and simple resolutions.

Step 1. The official legislative process begins when a bill or resolution is numbered — H.R. signifies a House bill and S. a Senate bill — and then referred to a committee and printed by the Government Printing Office.

Step 2. Referral to Committee: With few exceptions, bills are referred to standing committees in the House or Senate according to carefully delineated rules of procedure.

Step 3. Committee Action: When a bill reaches a committee, it is placed on the committee's calendar. A bill can be referred to a subcommittee or considered by the committee as a whole. It is at this point that a bill is examined carefully and its chances for passage are determined. If the committee does not act on a bill, it is the equivalent of killing it.

Step 4. Subcommittee Review: Often, bills are referred to a subcommittee for study and hearings. Hearings provide the opportunity to put on the record the views of the executive branch, experts, other public officials, and supporters and opponents of the legislation. Testimony can be given in person or submitted as a written statement.

Step 5. Mark Up: When the hearings are completed, the subcommittee may meet to "mark up" the bill — that is, make changes and amendments prior to recommending the bill to the full committee. If a subcommittee votes not to report legislation to the full committee, the bill dies.

Step 6. Committee Action to Report a Bill: After receiving a subcommittee's report on a bill, the full committee can conduct further study and hearings, or it can vote on the subcommittee's recommendations and any proposed amendments. The full committee then votes on its recommendation to the House or Senate. This procedure is called "ordering a bill reported."

Step 7. Publication of a Written Report: After a committee votes to have a bill reported, the committee chair instructs staff to prepare a written report on the bill. This report describes the intent and scope of the legislation, impact on existing laws and programs, the position of the executive branch, and views of dissenting members of the committee.

Step 8. Scheduling Floor Action: After a bill is reported back to the chamber where it originated, it is placed in chronological order on the calendar.

In the House, there are several different legislative calendars, and the Speaker and majority leader largely determine whether, when, and in what order bills come up. In the Senate, there is only one legislative calendar.

Step 9. Debate: When a bill reaches the floor of the House or Senate, there are rules or procedures governing the debate on the legislation. These rules determine the conditions and amount of time allocated for general debate.

Step 10. Voting: After the debate and the approval of any amendments, the bill is passed or defeated by the members voting.

Step 11. Referral to Other Chamber: When a bill is passed by the House or the Senate, it is referred to the other chamber, where it usually follows the same route through committee and floor action. This chamber may approve the bill as received, reject it, ignore it, or change it.

Step 12. Conference Committee Action: If only minor changes are made to a bill by the other chamber, it is common for the legislation to go back to the first chamber for concurrence. However, when the actions of the other chamber significantly alter the bill, a conference committee is formed to reconcile the differences between the House and Senate versions. If the conferees are unable to reach agreement, the legislation dies. If agreement is reached, a conference report is prepared describing the committee members' recommendations for changes. Both the House and the Senate must approve the conference report.

Step 13. Final Actions: After a bill has been approved by both the House and Senate in identical form, it is sent to the President. If the President signs the legislation, it becomes law. If the President takes no action for ten days while Congress is in session (excluding Sundays and the day it is received), the bill automatically becomes law—unless Congress prevents its return by adjourning. This is known as a "pocket veto." The President may also veto the bill and return it to Congress.

Step 14. Overriding a Veto: If the President vetoes the bill, Congress may attempt to override the veto. This requires a two-thirds roll call vote of sufficient numbers of members for a quorum.

A bill becomes law on the date of approval or passage over the President's veto, unless it expressly provides a different effective date. Each of the steps in the process provide an opportunity for advocacy, but the first step — the introduction of the bill to the respective chamber — provides the best opportunity. With each successive step, the process becomes more resistant to change.

DIRECT ADVOCACY BY TRUSTEES: WRITING OR E-MAILING MEMBERS OF CONGRESS

Although Representatives receive hundreds of letters and e-mails each week and Senators often receive hundreds each day, a thoughtful, concise personal letter or e-mail often can have a significant impact. Members of Congress are very aware of the positions their constituents hold. Many offices keep a daily count of how their mail and e-mail is running on particular issues. **Your letter/e-mail does matter.** Remember that trustees are seen by lawmakers as representing the very same constituencies and thus have great credibility among policymakers in Washington, D.C.

There are no shortcuts to good letters, whether hardcopy or electronic. Remember to keep letters and e-mails short and to the point. **Candor, conviction, relevant data, and personal anecdotes always help.** Examples drawn from campus or community programs can be very persuasive, but avoid strong emotion and exaggeration. **Factual information** is important to broadening support for legislative items.

Timing is an important factor. Try to write your position on a bill/issue while it is in committee. Your Representatives and Senators usually can be more responsive to your appeal at that time than when the bill has been reported out favorably by a committee for floor action.

Contact information for Representatives and Senators can be found on ACCT's Legislation Action Center under "Find Your Legislator."

Tips for an Effective Letter:

» Write on your college's stationery or on business or personal letterhead if you have a long-term relationship with your Senator or Representative.

» Make sure the spelling and address of the Senator/Representative are correct, and use the following format:

> The Honorable Joe Smith
> U.S. House of Representatives
> Washington, DC 20515
> Or
> The Honorable Joe Smith
> United States Senate
> Washington, DC 20510

» State the issue of concern and your position on the issue in the first sentence. Use this type of direct and to-the-point style throughout your letter. For example:

> "Dear Representative Smith:
> I urge you to support House Bill (H.R.) 123, as it will greatly affect the community I represent as a trustee at XYZ community college."

» Double-check bill numbers, sponsors' names, and the title of the bill.

» Make your case on one page. Be substantive, factual and concise. Tell how the legislation is likely to affect your community. Describe how it would also affect community college students in the Congressional district and your state.

» Convey your expert knowledge on community college issues. Representatives look to their expert constituents and consider their views when making decisions. Include the college's Web site and encourage the legislator to visit and learn more about the college and students.

» Respectfully request the Member's position on the issue, as well as a substantive reply.

» Extend an invitation to the Member of Congress to visit your college when he or she is in town. At minimum encourage them to visit the college's Web site as a way of seeing some of the great things going on at the college. The more personal contact you have with your Member of Congress, the more influence you will have on decisions. The better he or she knows you, the more your letter will stand out to your Member and his or her staff.

» Make sure your name, address, and e-mail are legible so that you may receive a reply as soon as possible.

» Both mail and e-mail copes of the letter.

» Send a copy of your letter to the ACCT Department of Public Policy. This assists staff in following up on issues with Congressional offices.

Additional Letter-Writing Tips from a Former Congressman:

The late Morris K. Udall, Congressman from Arizona, offered tips for communicating with Members of Congress in *The Congressional Record* in 1977. An edited version of his remarks follows:

DO

» Write your own views. A personal letter is far better than a form letter or a signature on a petition. I regret to report that form letters often receive form replies.

» Give your reasons for taking a stand.

» Be constructive.

» If you have expert knowledge, share it. I can't possibly be an expert in all fields. Many of my constituents are experts in some fields. I welcome their advice and counsel.

» Say "well done" when it's deserved. Congressmen are human too, and they appreciate an occasional "well done" from people who believe they have done the right thing. I know I do. But even if you think I went wrong on an issue, I would welcome a letter telling me you disagreed; it may help me on another issue later.

DON'T
» Don't make threats or promises.
» Don't berate your Congressman.
» Don't pretend to wield vast political influence.
» Don't become a constant "pen pal," writing on every issue being considered.

In summary, to be successful at the national level, it is imperative for boards and presidents to take advantage of all the tools and resources available. The list of priorities for the board should include active participation at the National Legislative Summit (NLS), annual visits to Senators' and Representatives' offices during NLS, and gathering as much information as possible to take back home. Sending out a press release with photographs of the visit with congressional representatives is an important part of the strategy. Promoting the image of trustees working on behalf of the college on Capitol Hill sends a valuable message to faculty, staff, students, and the community, reinforcing the important leadership and advocacy role of the board.

SAMPLE NATIONAL ADVOCACY ACTION PLAN

Activities/Events	Participants	Preparation/action/ Follow-up
Annual attendance at the National Legislative Summit (NLS), Washington, D.C.	All trustees, president, select students	• Visit congressional representatives • Identify priorities • Prepare position paper(s) • Issue press release before and after • Thank you letter
Design campus legislative visits • Legislative breakfast • Special events	All trustees, president, select students, faculty	• Tour of campus • Special presentations highlighting students and programs
Commencement • Invite as speakers • Acknowledge attendance by elected officials • Inform them how many students are graduating from their district	All trustees, president	• Organize a special reception for afterwards • Issue press releases acknowledging attendance
ACCT Alerts	President, trustees	Make calls • Send letters • Send e-mails
Promotional materials, special events	Public relations or government affairs office	• Include congressional, state, and local elected officials in mailing list to receive promotional materials • Provide brief quarterly memo on exciting things going on at the college
Relationship building	All trustees, president, public relations & government affairs, students and community	Attend activities being sponsored by legislators that support the well-being of the community such as health fairs.
During the election campaign • Issue educational position paper • Distribute to all candidates • Take advantage of opportunities to make case on behalf of education	Board, president, public relations or government affairs staff	Issue with a formal press release to all candidates

Advocacy in the 21st Century: Establishing a Forward-Thinking National Legislative Agenda

by Jee Hang Lee

Background

Federal and state legislators have always supported the important roles of community colleges in securing educational and economic prosperity for local communities. An important and organized display of support took place in 2005, when a small group of legislators led by Rep. Brad Miller (D-N.C.) created the House Community College Caucus. The creation of this caucus was a significant achievement for community colleges, their students, and their collective mission.

The following statement of purpose was developed during the creation of the House Community College Caucus:

> The Community College Caucus recognizes that community colleges play an important and distinctive role in the American education system. Community colleges provide a low-cost, close-to-home education to more than 11.6 million students a year. The ability of community colleges to adapt to the needs of the community situates them to play a key role in training workers in our evolving economy. The purpose of the CCC is to raise awareness within the House of Representatives about the unique role of community colleges within the American educational system. The Caucus will serve as a forum to identify and discuss current issues which affect community colleges.

The original co-chairs of the House Community College Caucus were Reps. Miller, Michael Castle (R-Del.), Roger Wicker (R-Miss.), and David Wu (D-Ore.).

After the unprecedented growth of the House Community College Caucus, community college leaders approached Sens. Ben Nelson (D-Neb.) and Richard Burr (R-N.C.) about beginning a Senate Community College Caucus. In 2007, Sens. Nelson and Burr officially began the caucus. In 2008, the co-chairmanship of the Senate caucus was expanded to include Sens. Blanche Lincoln (D-Ark.) and Roger Wicker (R-Miss.). With Sen. Wicker's move to the Senate, Rep. Tom Latham (R-Iowa) was added as a co-chair to the House Caucus.

Members of the House of Representatives and Senate have since taken significant steps to publicly demonstrate their strong support for community colleges by continuously expanding both Caucuses. This show of support not only increases the stature and importance of community colleges, but also opens the way for the nation's 1,170 community colleges to reach a new level in carrying out their legislative agenda in Washington, D.C.

Purpose and Process of Forming a Congressional Caucus

Typically, Congressional caucuses are formed by select members of Congress who support specific interests or common legislative positions. Both chambers of Congress can have caucuses. In general, caucuses range in size, with some made up of only a handful of members and others consisting of over 200 members. The House Democratic and Republican Caucuses are prime examples of how some caucuses are used. Each caucus has its own charter statement, which serves as its statement of purpose.

The Community College Caucuses focus on disseminating information about the positive contributions of community colleges and educating Members of Congress and congressional staffers. These efforts equip lawmakers and their staffers to support colleges in their districts and states. The Caucuses are now working on community college-focused legislation to build Congress' awareness of the issues confronting colleges.

The Community College Caucuses represent a significant achievement that will pay dividends in facilitating our advocacy work. The list of current members of the caucus can be found on the ACCT Web site at www.acct.org. If your congressional representatives have not yet joined, please urge them to do so.

Due to the positive outcomes of the House and Senate Caucuses, community college leaders have looked towards their state capitals to develop similar caucuses. Texas is an example of a state that has incorporated this model at the state level. As the Congressional Community College Caucuses grow, college leaders should take advantage of this effort to strengthen and build legislative support for community colleges by mobilizing their trustees, colleges, and association to visit and support community colleges.

TODAY'S COMMUNITY COLLEGE LEGISLATIVE AGENDA

Historically and due to the nature of the federal and state legislative and budgetary processes, ACCT, AACC, and community colleges across the country have been focused on short-term annual efforts, or the "here-and-now" approach to the federal budget and appropriations process. This annual process ensures that ACCT, AACC, and colleges spend time and resources to affect the legislative process each year. Each year, ACCT, on behalf of governing boards throughout the country, renews its fight for an equitable piece of the federal appropriations funding pie for community colleges. ACCT supports the community college movement by supporting a larger effort to increase college access and affordability.

Overall, the method that the federal government provides for higher education budgeting and appropriations makes it difficult for ACCT to specifically target funding toward community colleges. In elementary and secondary education, school districts, not students, receive federal dollars. But the largest higher education program, the Pell Grant program, distributes funds directly to students, who in turn determine their own higher education destinations. Currently, more than 2 million community college students receive a Pell Grant each year. While Pell Grant funds are not allocated directly to community colleges, the funds help students attend our colleges. Programs such as the Pell Grant are critical for the vitality of higher education. ACCT advocates for the Pell Grant program because the program directly supports community college students and indirectly supports community colleges.

As ACCT works with other national associations, advocacy groups, and colleges, one of our greatest activities related to the appropriations process is to ensure that the funding level at least matches the previous year's level. If not, programs may be at risk of losing significant amounts of funding or may even be eliminated outright. The appropriations process is volatile and potentially treacherous because it is tied in with the annual federal budgetary process. The budget is different each year, which can result in funding disparities for various federal agencies and programs, ultimately affecting community colleges.

Understanding the Congressional calendar is a significant factor in ACCT's legislative success. During election years, the legislative workload of Congress typically declines. This is due to the reduction of work days in Washington, D.C. so Members of Congress can be in their home states while campaigning for re-election. The limited number of active Congressional days also results in Congress only dealing with must-pass pieces of legislation, such as appropriations bills. The federal government cannot operate without appropriations bills. But in many instances, programs and agencies can continue to carry out their duties without an authorization bill.

The absence of key reauthorization bills, which authorize pieces of legislation affecting many federal programs, further complicates the Congressional calendar. ACCT and others have great difficulty prioritizing their shared legislative agenda around political discourse without a legislative vehicle through which to push. For example, the passage of the Higher Education Opportunity Act (also known as the reauthorization of the Higher Education Act) in 2008 means that Congress will not look again at the reauthorization of HEA until 2014. Although the Act is expected to expire in 2014, it is very likely that Congress will simply extend the existing Act for a period of time. It took Congress six years and fourteen extensions to complete a comprehensive reauthorization of HEA. Now that the HEA reauthorization has passed, ACCT will collaborate with the Department of Education as it implements the provisions within the bill.

One of the universal truths of about advocacy in Washington, D.C. is that advocacy efforts are in many ways focused on maintaining and protecting provisions and programs that organizations support. Many federal programs are critical to our colleges. Some provide financial assistance directly to students, and many support funding for staff and equipment. ACCT and community colleges work constantly to maintain key programs and provisions that community colleges support.

A good example of this type of scenario occurred during the 109th Congress, when the reauthorization of the Carl D. Perkins Act was up for consideration and there was an effort to consolidate several programs because of the perceived belief that they were duplicative in nature. At the same time, the funding for Perkins programs was slated for consolidation. A strong bi-partisan advocacy effort was needed to ensure that the Perkins programs were reauthorized and their funding restored. In many instances, organizations and others build coalitions to fight to maintain the gains that were achieved over many years.

Targeted Funding or "Earmarks"

In some instances, community colleges work to build federal support around a funding priority within the college. Community colleges from across the country work with their Congressional representatives and delegations to pursue funding through "earmarks," congressionally directed funding for projects and programs. These "earmarks" support targeted efforts such as equipment for a nursing or first responder program. The earmark process mirrors the appropriations process, and community colleges must work to get access to these highly competitive funds. Colleges must do a significant amount of legwork, such as working with partners to garner support, and prepare for the process a year ahead of the actual request. While Congress may pass thousands of earmarks each year, it typically receives four to five times more requests than they fund.

FORWARD THINKING FOR COMMUNITY COLLEGE ADVOCACY

Now that we have the support of one of the largest and most diverse caucuses, community colleges need to capitalize on the growth and diversity of the caucus membership in order to effect favorable changes. The growth of the Congressional Community College Caucuses opens the door for ACCT, AACC, and community colleges across the country to develop a forward-thinking legislative agenda that will help our institutions compete in the 21st century. The caucuses have a built-in constituency that supports the community college mission and which we anticipate will be leveraged to support a long-term agenda focused on critical needs.

Now more than ever, community colleges must do more with limited resources. Countless communities look to community colleges to provide students and communities with higher education, adult education, job training, and other needs as necessary. One only need look at a community college class schedule to see the breadth of courses offered by our institutions. With community colleges working to meet all of the demands within a local community, the federal and state governments need to step up to the plate to support our colleges. As we look to the future, three key issues appear on the horizon for community colleges.

1. Investing in Community College Infrastructure

When considering that community colleges comprise the largest sector of higher education and one of the largest economic engines in the economy, it is unacceptable that college facilities are bursting at the seams. Community college enrollment continues to grow each year, which compounds the problem and exacerbates the need to replace and/or retrofit facilities.

Historically, the federal government provided funding and tax benefits to allow community colleges to build the necessary infrastructure. But the federal government has not been an active partner in this effort over the past couple of decades. As communities and the federal government rely more heavily on community colleges, the federal government needs to take an active role in ensuring that community colleges are equipped to deal with the upcoming challenges.

2. Community Colleges as Community-Based Economic Engines

The growing emphasis on the community college as an economic development center creates new opportunities. But along with opportunities come a number of challenges, including having the resources to develop new training programs in high-cost technical and health fields and sustainable, or "green," efforts.

As community colleges have changed with the times to meet the demands of the community, so has the way the government looks at and works with community colleges. One recent federal program of note is the Community Based Job Training Grant program. This program offers competitive grant funds to community colleges to help colleges provide job training around high-need and high-demand positions. With CBJTG funded at $125 million annually, community colleges need access to more programs like CBJTG — or the funding for CBJTG needs to be increased.

3. Investing in Combating Poverty and Improving Equity through Community College Education

As the U.S. economy becomes more of a global economy, international competition has resulted in significant ramifications, from plant closures to full industries being consolidated or outsourced. The overall effect is that poverty continues to grow and is becoming more difficult to overcome. As the nation works to alleviate poverty, community colleges are on the front line of the fight to ensure that each individual has the education and training to be able to find a job that provides a livable wage.

In the 21st Century, there are increasing requirements for workers of today and tomorrow. According to a 2007 report by Jobs for the Future, *Hitting Home: Quality, Cost, and Access Challenges Confronting Higher Education Today,* the United States will need to produce 15.6 million more bachelor's and associate's degrees beyond currently expected levels if the nation is to keep up with its best-performing peers. This daunting task can only be accomplished if community colleges are active participants in this endeavor. Unfortunately, the education gap continues to grow each year and will not likely reverse itself. Furthermore, a 2006 U.S. Bureau of Labor Statistics study notes that education and training demands for employment are growing with the changing U.S. economy.

According to the U.S. Census Bureau 2007 American Community Survey, more than 70 percent of people living below the poverty line are high school graduates (equivalent) or less than high school graduates. From a purely economic sense, an individual who has an associate's degree on average earns $39,724, while a high school graduate earns $31,071 and a high school dropout earns $20,901, according to Census figures. Over a lifetime, an individual with an associate's degree will earn over $300,000 more than a high-school graduate.

Federal and state legislators need to work with community colleges to build awareness around this important factor and build a set of programs to provide the financial support and incentives to encourage all citizens to attain higher education. A working individual brings in tax revenue, thereby decreasing the social cost of the individual to the government and yeilding social savings including "costs stemming from reductions in incarceration, welfare, health care support, and others" (The Economic Contribution of America's Technical and Community Colleges, EMSI, 2004).

While legislators and the public need to look at educational attainment, there also needs to be a focus on lifelong learning and adult education. One of the fastest-growing student populations for community colleges is individuals who hold higher education degrees. Community colleges are working with these individuals to provide them with the mobility to change jobs. As we know, local economies will continuously remake themselves as new industries emerge, and community colleges are there to keep up with workforce needs of the community, and to ensure the economic vitality of the local communities that they serve.

As the country and local communities work to compete in a global economy, community colleges must be engaged and supported as the economic engines that they are in order to maximize the results and ultimately help individuals and communities to strive and succeed in this ever-changing economy.

Jee Hang Lee is the director of public policy
for the Association of Community College Trustees.

Effective Advocacy at the State and Local Levels

The success of a state advocacy effort is not possible without the full cooperation of all parties involved in the community college network. All the community voices must be heard above the other special interest voices that compete for state dollars.

KEY TO EFFECTIVE ADVOCACY: STRATEGIC DEVELOPMENT OF THE ADVOCACY MESSAGE

The president of the college typically prepares and discusses the legislative and advocacy priorities with the board. This is a healthy approach to make sure all trustees are on board, have a common agenda, and can develop an effective communication strategy. It is always important to remember that legislators have many constituencies with competing interests pressuring for their own causes. Building a forceful and powerful voice on behalf of the college requires discipline, focus, and the effective articulation of a clear and relevant message.

The advocacy message should be simple, short, relevant, and clear. It should be a consistent message that focuses on inspiring your legislator to take supportive action. How and when the advocacy message is delivered is equally important. Know the schedule for key committee decisions on bills or the authorization of allocations. Legislators like to invest in successful ventures that can influence their positive standing within the communities they represent. The more visible and valued the college is within the community, the more receptive legislators will be to requests for support. (This, of course, underscores the importance of effective public and media relations within your college's community.)

Some colleges develop a strategic approach to building legislative support. These efforts are enhanced when trustees and presidents understand the importance of institutional visibility as defined by a positive relationship with the community, positive media coverage, and long-term relationships with key elected officials. A sample advocacy/relationship plan or checklist could include the following components:

STATE ADVOCACY/RELATIONSHIP PLAN				
Priorities (funding, capital projects, etc.)	Key Legislators to be Targeted	Public/ Community Perception	Targeted Activities' Media Coverage	Advocacy team, Champions & Spokesperson
Prepare materials, reports, and dates in support of priorities	Develop brief profile on each	Work to maintain a good relationship with the community	Create events, opportunities for coverage and getting the message out	Participate in key state and local gatherings Participate in "state of the state" message by the governor

THE IMPORTANCE OF A COMPETITIVE STATE ADVOCACY TEAM

A well-organized state advocacy team must be competitive. There are just as many advocacy groups out there as there are issues, all competing for the same scarce state dollars. Because states must balance their budgets every year, institutions that depend on state-level funding must be strategically positioned as a priority to local legislators.

Trustees, working at the state level, must bring legislators to the point where they will champion the community college cause over other pressing state needs. It's not enough to state the merits of the community college. Noble documentation is not enough when community colleges are competing with other groups that are just as sincere and just as well documented. Community college trustees must make their voices of their communities clearly heard and heeded.

Funding sources for community colleges vary widely across states, ranging from municipalities to counties to states, and from property taxes to state appropriations. The vast majority of community colleges, however, obtain an important part of their funding from the state. Consequently, state legislatures must absolutely be a major focus of community college advocacy efforts.

Community colleges face fierce competition for the attention of state and local legislators and policymakers, and the competition for more public dollars is especially fierce. Fortunately, the legislative process is substantially similar in Congress and state legislatures. All but one state (Nebraska) have bicameral legislatures and committees similar to those in Congress. Many of the same strategies used at the national level apply to advocacy at the local and state levels. Effective advocacy at the state level requires knowing the issues, being armed with good information, getting to know your legislators and making yourself and your college known to them, staying in touch with them and, at the appropriate time, making a clear, cogent statement on the policy or legislation in question and requesting their support.

And then the process begins again with the next issue — or the next legislative session. As with all good relationships, the advocate-legislator relationship needs care and nurturing, including regular, clear communication, listening to one another, honesty, transparency, and appreciating each other's contributions. With politicians, the expressions of appreciation, if possible, should be done publicly. They appreciate the good publicity.

THE ROLE OF TRUSTEES AND THE PRESIDENT

The Role of Trustees

Trustees have an essential role as part of a state advocacy team effort. They represent the "community" in "community college." Trustees are elected or appointed on the basis of their ties to and involvement with their community. Trustees are a key link in the two-way communication between the community college and the state capital. The two most important qualities a trustee has to offer to legislative advocacy are that trustees, as community leaders, can effectively promote the college as a community resource and help marshal community support for college legislative priorities. Who better than a trustee to advocate for community college priorities?

The ultimate key to successful legislative relations is the manner by which the local board carries out its duties and responsibilities. Good trusteeship and its "ripple effect" in the capital support successful legislative advocacy. To assure legislative effectiveness, the community college board should establish policy advocacy as a top priority for the college and see to it that public policy issues are discussed at every board meeting. They should work with the college president to set the legislative agenda for the college, and they must become very familiar with that agenda. The college president is the quarterback on the college's advocacy team, and the trustees are essential team members. This helps ensure that everyone on the team carries the same message to legislators.

The Role of the President

The president is responsible for establishing the climate for legislative advocacy on campus. One of the president's important duties during the legislative session is to make advocacy activities, both on- and off-campus, a top priority. Presidents should "quarterback" their campus legislative action program, orchestrating, delegating, and monitoring activities for maximum effectiveness. Presidents should work in partnership with a campus Legislative Action Team (more on this below), giving direction, setting the tone on campus, and providing coordination of the legislative activities schedule. Presidents provide expertise that the system needs to effectively explain community college issues to the legislature. Participating in committee hearings and in small group meetings with legislative leaders and staff strengthens the community colleges' legislative effectiveness.

An important role for the president is to make advocacy activity a top priority for the college staff, professors, and students, all of whom should be represented on the team. While he or she must delegate the actual day-to-day chores of advocacy to staff, the president sets the direction for the Legislative Action Team, sets the campus tone, and checks in with the team regularly. The president and trustees are the most likely candidates to visit legislators and testify at public hearings on legislation or policy matters. Their presence and commitment conveys to the legislators the importance of the legislation or issue to their shared constituents and communities.

BUILDING ON GOODWILL AND PUBLIC PERCEPTION

Public opinion surveys show that community college education enjoys broad public support. The principal task of the legislative advocacy program is to translate that public support into legislative votes. That requires three principal areas of effort:
» Organizing the Legislative Action Team;
» Identifying "friends" of the college within the community and translating their support into legislative advocacy; and,
» Developing a strong relationship with local media.

The task for both the Legislative Action Team and community supporters is to make community colleges a part of each legislator's thinking and relevant to their agendas, as well as to connect the colleges' needs to legislators' needs. Involving legislators in the means to achieving community college goals makes them a part of the community college movement and allows them to take a well-deserved bow in a public arena.

It is not enough for a select few to deal just with legislative leaders; more people have to deal with all members of the legislature. Widespread interaction must come from all legislative districts to have the level of influence that results in support at the state level.

THE IMPORTANCE OF PERSISTENCE

Elected officials respond to constituents who hold influence within the community and who make a concerted and frequent effort to establish and nurture two-way relationships. Winning or losing a legislative effort can depend on trustee participation. Steady, constructive pressure and constant feedback — regular letters or e-mails, a steady barrage of friendly but urgent phone calls, a steady stream of concerned and informed visitors to the capital — gets the job done. Avoid the "big burst" — only writing or calling to make a request without already having established a relationship or followed through with a promised action. The "winner" is the one who makes the best-organized, most effective, and most persistent effort. Effective advocacy is ongoing, day-to-day pressure on behalf of community colleges, which proves that the people care about their colleges and the things they do — that the state cannot get along without community colleges, and that community colleges need state support to survive and thrive. The goal is to get firm support to bring legislators to the point at which, during a crisis, a strong majority says: "Community colleges? You bet we support them; they are a top priority!" The goal of effective advocacy is to make this sentiment second-nature. When this sentiment becomes second-nature, legislators will show their support through financial and legislative support.

Three things to always remember:
- » Legislators relate to their local colleges.
- » Legislators must understand the role and priorities of the community college system before they arrive in the capital for the session.
- » Legislators want to be identified with success.

Sources of advocacy efforts for community college legislative priorities vary from state to state. They may include the staff of a state board for community college education and/or staff of one or more state associations for trustees, presidents, or related office-holders. But the basic foundation for promoting legislative priorities must be local college Legislative Action Teams collaborating and working together to represent all regions of the state. These teams can hold the key to success or failure of the entire state program.

Remember, the keys to effective advocacy are your college, your campus, and your community. If each trustee and each Legislative Action Team makes a firm commitment and persists in their efforts to get the job done, community colleges can achieve a highly effective legislative advocacy network.

ORGANIZING THE TEAM FOR STATE-WIDE OR REGIONAL ADVOCACY

Legislators are most interested in the needs of their own constituents. Therefore, the best way to get a message across is by organizing concerted communication among and from local constituents. Obtain a legislative district map from the county auditor to locate team members in the district by their home addresses. Then, organize subgroups of the team according to legislative districts, even if they may not coincide perfectly with the college's service area. This type of communication network facilitates quick action and will deliver a strong message to legislators when necessary. (Remember that there is strength in numbers.)

On the local level, there should be both an on-campus and an off-campus Legislative Action Team. These teams work to help legislators understand the college's needs within the context of state-wide community college needs. The on-campus team should include trustees, presidents, public information officers, students and their government leaders, faculty, representatives of labor organizations, alumni, staff, advisory committee members, and foundation board members. The off-campus team should include opinion leaders, members of civic associations, corporations, small businesses, and representatives from other education sectors, including all levels, from K-12 to colleges and universities.

Determine how individuals with special relationships with legislators can leverage those relationships on behalf of the campus. Know the best person to contact legislators in "a pinch." This will usually be someone who knows the legislator personally or a prominent community or business leader. It is typically the president's role to build strong and credible relationships with elected officials and their staff. That said, trustees can and should exert influence whenever necessary and appropriate.

Other key steps to organizing these teams include:

» **Selecting chairpersons.** These can include the president, a designee, or a trustee to represent the on-campus team. A community or business leader should represent the off-campus team.

» **Determining the contact on campus for the teams.** This could be the president or the person in charge of public policy.

» **Using technology** to set up a communications network. Technology has reduced the need for face-to-face meetings, travel time, and telephone tag. Use an e-mail distribution list to rapidly disseminate information to team members, send action alerts, and monitor action and report back results and information by legislative district. Online forums, search engines, blogs, and government Web sites can be good sources of information. Be sure to sign up for ACCT's Latest Action in Washington E-Alerts, which can be forwarded among your electronic distribution list to keep team members informed. To sign up, send an e-mail to publicpolicy@ acct.org with "LAW E-Alert" in the subject line.

Teams can be the key to the success or failure of your college's legislative program. Don't forget to thank all members of your team for each task they perform and at the end of the legislative session — win or lose. Communication efforts should be constant and ongoing regardless of the outcome, as should your gratitude for everyone's positive efforts.

THE ACTION PLAN

An action plan will provide a framework for your teams. The plan will help the president organize campus strategy — jobs to be done, responsible person(s), and a timeframe for the work. These tasks should be organized by legislative district. Many states have state organizations whose primary responsibility is to coordinate the state-wide advocacy effort. The legislative session should be put into the annual calendar and it should be given top priority.

Voter Registration Efforts – Demonstrating Campus-Wide Civic Responsibility

Remind campus groups and individuals to update their voter registrations and to vote. Hold a voter-registration drive on campus, using students and faculty. Encourage voting within the pages of campus publications and newsletters, and on posters displayed around campus. Elected officials are very interested in helping groups that can affect election outcomes — and college campuses represent thousands — or tens of thousands — of motivated voters.

Before, During, and After a Legislative Session

Develop a pre-session activities checklist. This will organize your Legislative Action Team's efforts and ensure that all necessary steps are taken in order to best influence public policy decisions that affect your college or colleges.

Pre-session Checklist:

- Develop the community college system's priorities for the upcoming session of the legislature. The Legislative Action Team can work with state associations and/or the state board to help decide what issues on funding, program implementation, and regulations that the community colleges will pursue that legislative year.
- Before the primary election, send each candidate an information packet on the college. This packet should include a letter of introduction, a college fact sheet, and an open invitation to visit the campus.
- After the primary, contact the nominated candidate and extend a formal invitation to visit the campus. Provide a tour of the campus while it is busy (don't forget evening programs), and encourage the use of college facilities for the candidate's meetings and public forums. Provide as much information on the college as possible, organized by legislative district. For example, offer data that show student enrollment, participation in financial aid, demographics, and courses studied by legislative district.
- Following the election, meet with your legislative delegation (preferably one at a time) to discuss the college or college system's legislative priorities. One-on-one meetings are generally more effective than group meetings. Be sure to show your college's portion of the budget request (or budget cuts) and translate dollars into services. Be sure to show legislative district enrollments.
- Develop a central information bank. Compile a list of campus and community members who can help with a legislator. Determine who helped on campaigns and who is close to the legislators in your district.
- Develop a Legislative Action Team within each legislative district that can respond when needed with letters, phone calls, visits to the capital, etc.
- Promote public awareness of the college and its services to the community. Such activities could include:
  - » inviting community groups to meet on campus;
  - » providing speakers (trustees, presidents, and other staff) to community groups;
  - » writing news stories about the college and its students; and
  - » publicizing news stories that publicize the economic impact of the college within its community.
- Notify legislators of achievements made by students and staff from their legislative district, such as scholarships, contest winners, faculty awards, etc. Put your legislators on your mailing list so that they are informed about all college events.
- Support the president's efforts to build relationships with legislators by understanding the time it takes and the need to be visible in the state's capital.

During the Session:

- **The Legislative Branch**
  Know the structure and organization of the state legislature. Obtain lists of legislative session leaders and committee memberships. Identify the legislators from your community college district who serve in leadership positions and on key committees.
- **Committee Assignments**
  Lists of committee assignments are available from the legislature at the beginning of each session. Find out who among your legislators is assigned to committees that handle community college legislation (i.e., Higher Education, Appropriations, Ways and Means, etc.). If one or more of your legislators is assigned to committees dealing directly with community colleges, write to them and let them know that you are pleased with their assignment and look forward to working with them in support of community colleges. Whenever possible, arrange to sit in on a committee hearing or two, and introduce yourself before or after the hearing. This "makes your presence known" and shows that you are an interested party who is watching after community college interests. The informal introductions and visits with legislators before and after hearings are an excellent way to reinforce the community college presence.

  Another way of reinforcing community college advocacy efforts is to testify during a committee hearing on a community college issue. Simply making the effort to show up and speak up can be an effective form of advocacy, and sharing firsthand experiences on the record can make a great impression on legislators.
- **Track Key Legislation**
  There are a number of sources for tracking legislation, ranging from newspapers and legislative news bulletins published by various interest groups to keeping in constant contact with key staff members responsible for the legislation and your state association.
- **Translate College Data into Legislative District Data**
  For example, show college enrollment in terms of legislative district enrollment. Your legislators want to know how legislation will impact the colleges in their districts.
- **Visit the Capital**
  When you can, coordinate your visits with other college advocacy groups so that there are community college people in the legislative halls every week of the session. Legislators are most available at the beginning of the session. As the deadlines for bill action and budget votes loom, it becomes exceedingly difficult to reach legislators personally.

  Unfortunately, there is no "best time" to reach your members in the capital. Many legislators find early morning breakfast meetings convenient, while others prefer quick lunch meetings and still others like late evening dinners after a long day. Some will schedule you for ten minutes before or after committee hearings. Be flexible and work with your member's preferred schedule; the easier you make it for him or her to meet with you, the more receptive he or she will be. When you do meet, visit the capital as a two-part team: one part from the college — the president, trustees, faculty, students, graduates — and one part from the community — mayors, county commissioners, and business leaders. After the meeting, debrief. What do you think your legislator told you? Where do you stand after the visit? What are the next steps? Provide your fellow advocacy organizations with feedback, including comments that may seem relatively unimportant. All information is vital to the formulation of positions and strategy.

- **When Called Upon, Make the Contacts with Legislators**
  When legislative action alerts are issued by the college, it is your responsibility as a member of the team to make the phone call or write the letter. Be sure you are briefed on the issue before you make the legislative contact, and be prepared to answer questions should they arise.
- **Visit Legislators at Home**
  Most legislators return to their homes each weekend during a session, and they often make public appearances within their districts. When they do, make a point of attending these appearances and introducing yourself to the legislator. Put in a good word for the community college legislative program.
- **Prepare a Schedule for Letter Writing, Phone Calls, and Visits to the Capital**
- **Share feedback with others** working on the issues, such as the state board, associations, and lobbyists.

Post-Session Activities:

- Debrief. Hold a post-mortem on what worked and didn't work during the session.
- Modify the college's Legislative Action Team and alter strategy to reflect needs identified in the post-mortem.
- Publicly and privately thank local legislators who supported community colleges.
- Stay in touch with your legislators during the off-season; build continuing relationships.
- Acknowledge the key role of the president and support his or her efforts.
- Participate in "legislative days" and/or receptions, as well as activities sponsored by state associations.

PERSONAL PERSPECTIVE
Trustee Advocacy at the State Level: The Minnesota Experience

By David C. Olson and James H. McCormick

Trustees can play a critical role as advocates for their colleges. In Minnesota, advocacy and outreach by the 15-member Board of Trustees of the Minnesota State Colleges and Universities system are central to the system's success. The system comprises 25 community and technical colleges and seven state universities located on 54 campuses across the state. It was formed by the 1995 merger of the state's community college system, technical college system, and state university system, each of which had its own governing board and chancellor. The system now operates with one board and one chancellor. Serving nearly 390,000 students in credit and non-credit courses a year, the Minnesota State Colleges and Universities system is the nation's fifth-largest system of two and four-year colleges and universities.

Trustees are appointed by the governor and approved by the state Senate. Twelve trustees serve six-year terms; one trustee is appointed from each of the state's eight congressional districts, and four are appointed from the state at large. Three student trustees, one each from the state universities, technical colleges, and community colleges, serve two-year terms. Trustees advocate for all of the colleges and universities in the system, not just those located in their home districts.

Typical for most in the higher education arena, trustees are responsible for policies directly related to system planning, academic programs, fiscal management, personnel, admissions requirements, tuition and fees, and rules and regulations. The board also appoints the system's chancellor and presidents of the colleges and universities.

Within that framework, certain basics of a smooth-functioning higher education system or college must be in place before trustees are likely to accept the responsibility of the advocate. Trustees need to feel comfortable in their board position, fully owning their role as system leaders. This requires a commitment that often involves many hours of meetings and campus visits, in addition to preparing for meetings.

At the same time, the senior management team must take on the duty of being accountable to the board. Long-time higher education executives should avoid falling into the trap of believing they know all the answers. Given the seemingly intractable issues facing higher education across the country — low graduation rates, burdensome student debt loads, and disparities in achievement — it's clear no easy fixes are available.

Administrators need to be open to ideas and the perspectives of trustees.

The chancellor's role is to create the environment for constructive conversations between the board and management team. In Minnesota, the chancellor follows a simple rule-of-thumb in the Minnesota system: "make what is good better." The governing board is respected and valued. Staffing, good communications, and viable policy options provide a foundation for supporting these trustees as system advocates.

Advocacy does not mean that trustees avoid talking about institutional weaknesses or that they agree with every board policy or direction. Very often, a healthy tension can and should exist between trustees and the senior management team. Disagreements, however, are handled in a constructive and thoughtful manner.

Once these basics are in place, trustees are more likely to embrace advocacy. But what does it take to be an advocate for a college or higher education system?

Strong advocacy starts with well-informed trustees. To that end, trustees recently developed and launched a public online Accountability Dashboard. Though the system has been submitting accountability reports to the Legislature since 2001, trustees concluded in February 2007 that they wanted a public, easy-to-use tool that would display progress on specific performance measures for the 32 individual colleges and universities, as well as the system as a whole. Trustees made clear they wanted an honest assessment and didn't want to sugarcoat any weaknesses.

A committee of four trustees, four presidents, and four system office executives was formed to direct the dashboard's development over 18 months. Presidents raised concerns that such a public display of institutional performance would draw undue attention to weaknesses while ignoring institutional strengths. Trustees and others listened. Eventually, most concerns were allayed by including contextual information on the dashboard.

The board's involvement was key here. Periodic progress reports on the dashboard's development were presented to the full board. Trustees resisted pressure to add more than 10 performance measures on the advice of an expert who advised them to keep it simple. Indeed, if trustees hadn't been so directly involved, they might not have been as secure with the final product.

The dashboard, available at www.mnscu.edu (click on "Accountability" in the right column), provides a valuable tool for trustees' advocacy efforts. For the system, it is a visible demonstration of the board's commitment to continuous improvement. Online accessibility to the dashboard also assures the public that the trustees are holding the chancellor and the college and university presidents accountable for the results they produce. Such candor provides trustees with a way to acknowledge they are not satisfied with simply having a good system. They want to make it better.

In guiding system improvements, the trustees played the lead role in shaping the system's four-pronged strategic plan to drive access, program excellence, economic vitality, and innovation. As advocates, trustees took the plan to the executive and legislative branches and secured state funding for all four initiatives.

Effective advocates also take the public pulse. As representatives of 5 million Minnesotans, the system's trustees are well situated to do this. They typically hold other leadership positions or have other kinds of local, regional or statewide stature. Every day, they are out in their communities. Inevitably, they encounter dozens — maybe hundreds — of people in their lives. Many of these encounters generate feedback as people share their perceptions about what works and what doesn't work at the colleges and universities. Thus, trustees, like the proverbial canaries in the coal mine can pick up early warning signs of issues. Kudos from the public is a bonus, of course.

The three trustees who are students bring an additional perspective. They see and hear the concerns of their fellow students and can bring that feedback directly to the board. By informing the management team of these perceptions, trustees can provide insights that otherwise might be missed. Though community colleges historically have been more in touch with their local communities than large research-oriented universities, higher education administrators can lose sight of public perceptions about their institutions because daily demands of their jobs focus so much of their attention on internal campus issues.

A caveat is in order, however. Colleges and higher education systems — and ultimately students — are best served when the "listening" by trustees reaches far and wide. In other words, they can't just listen to business, or to students, or their friends. To be effective advocates, trustees seek connections to a wide range of constituencies to provide a balanced and fair reflection of public perceptions.

Trustees also can be advocates by building awareness and appreciation for the colleges among citizens and legislators. Prime opportunities arise when trustees address local chambers of commerce, service organizations, college advisory groups, or other public gatherings.

Though trustees have the freedom to express their opinions, they need to know how important it is to be consistent with the message of the system's strategic communications plan. One message which plays well with this system's trustees is reminding the public that the 32 institutions contribute mightily to the economic and social vitality of their communities and the state at large. In fact, an economic analysis showed that for every dollar in net state appropriation, the system returns $10.87 to the state's economy. It's also easy for trustees to embrace another key system message: We offer students more choices, better value, and unlimited possibilities.

The notion of trustees as advocates goes hand-in-hand with trustees as keepers of the system's legacy. Through their words and actions, trustees can have enormous influence with the state's political and business leaders, as well as the faculty, staff, and students in our colleges and universities.

David C. Olson is chair of the board of trustees
of the Minnesota State Colleges and Universities System.
He is also president of the Minnesota Chamber of Commerce.

James H. McCormick is the chancellor of the
Minnesota State Colleges and Universities System.

PERSONAL PERSPECTIVES
Trustee Advocacy at the State Level: The Texas Experience

By Kitty Boyle

In 1996 I was first elected to serve as a trustee for Dallas Community College District and what an experience it has been. In addition to the challenges of serving on our board, as our college has been a longtime member of ACCT, I have had the opportunity to attend all of ACCT's Annual Congress and National Legislative Summit meetings since becoming a trustee. The ACCT meetings have given me the rewarding experience of meeting trustees from across the nation who bring a wealth of commitment, knowledge, and dedication to the cause of our colleges. By providing a forum to discuss issues with other trustees from Texas, these meetings gave me a greater awareness of the issues regarding our state's community colleges.

In Texas, our colleges have for some years faced decreased state funding. The amount of money for our colleges in our state's budget has increased; however, the amount has not grown in keeping with our ever-increasing student enrollment. This has been a prominent discussion item among our Texas trustees and, as a result, an interest was formed in creating a trustee organization in Texas. After the 80th legislative session, a map printed in one of the community college publications showed on each state the percentage increase in funds that state had received during the legislative session. While serving on the ACCT board and executive committee, recognition of those states with strong trustee organizations was apparent and in looking at the map it was also apparent that those states with strong trustee organizations fared the best with their legislative budgets.

Also, during the time I served on the ACCT Executive Committee, national caucuses for community colleges were formed through the hard work of board members and trustees across the nation. I would be negligent not to mention that Pete Sercer from Midlands Technical College in South Carolina was and is instrumental in seeing to the success of the national caucuses, being intensely committed and dedicated. Witnessing the success of these caucuses, I contacted our local state representative and sought her assistance in forming community college caucuses in the Texas legislature. She was most helpful in obtaining a state senator to chair the caucus in the senate and a representative from the other party to co-chair the caucus in the house. A letter and form were created seeking the legislators' consent to join the caucuses, as was an attachment with statistics showing the growth of community colleges in our state, their importance to the workforce needs particularly in the health and emergency needs fields, and the overall economic importance of our colleges to our state and its citizens. The constant emphasis in our communications has been and is the economic impact of our colleges. A number of trustees who expressed an interest in a state organization were asked to sign their names on these request letters so that the legislators would know that this effort came from a wide variety of locations across the state and from colleges of all shapes and sizes.

At the same time the caucuses were developing, the interest in a state trustee organization was becoming more intense and many of the same trustees who had participated in the success of the state legislative caucuses began serious work on forming such an organization. While our organization was not fully up and running for the 81st legislative session, it was well on its way and we were a presence in the capitol. Many trustees were helpful with these efforts and I would like to mention our first officers and some of their numerous contributions.

Roberto Zarate from the Alamo Community College District served as our first chair. He was a signer of the initial caucus letters, made many trips to Austin, was instrumental in obtaining caucus members, hosted some of our meetings, had details such as minutes, notices, etc., taken care of, was invited to testify before the Workforce and gave testimony to the Legislative Budget Board.

Allen Kaplan from Austin Community College served as treasurer and was a signer of the initial caucus letters on which he wrote numerous personal notes, made many trips to the capitol, kept us informed regarding legislative happenings, had his college generously hold several of our meetings, put us in touch with a fellow trustee of his who drafted our bylaws, articles of incorporation, etc., testified before the Legislative Budget Board and the Senate Higher Education Committee and was a wealth of sound legislative advice. Being in the Austin area, Allen has been called for a variety of causes and has never failed to accomplish what was asked and has been a constantly steady support.

Chris Adler from Del Mar College served as secretary (she is no longer a trustee as she was elected to serve on the City Council in May), and she came up with an idea that has called much attention to our cause and has gotten our message more clearly across than otherwise would have been possible. We had circular red "stickies" made with a bright yellow line diagonally across the middle with 55% on one side of the line and 12% on the other. The 55% represented the percentage of Texas students in higher education and 12% represented the percentage of state higher-education dollars allocated to community colleges. Both of those percentages were very conservative. There is a "student day" at the capitol at the beginning of the legislative session and a large number of students wore those stickies and could easily tell the legislators they visited with what those numbers represented. The stickies were a great way to initiate discussion of our colleges' needs in our legislators offices, in the halls, in the elevators, and on our mail outs. One Senator took a stickie from one of us and wore it to the Budget Hearing. We are now rapidly approaching 60% of students in public higher education in Texas. Enrollment in community colleges nationally has been reported to be increasing at more than three time the rate of four year colleges and the growth is even greater in our State.

Molly Beth Malcolm from Texarkana College is now serving as treasurer and has invaluable contacts with legislators, having served as the state party chair a short while ago. She came back from the national convention with the signature of every Texas legislator who attended the convention on a caucus membership form. She spurs us on and is ever efficient in keeping us in order.

Hunter Ellington, a past trustee at Austin, has created a Web site for us. He indicates that it is possible to trace which persons who vote on a regular basis have attended Austin College. The possibilities of the extension of this idea are breathtaking to conceive.

There are now 125 members of the caucus in the house out of 150 members and 26 out of 31 members in the senate. With each legislative session there are changes in the members so this is, of course, an ongoing project. We know that more legislators than ever before can recognize a person as a community college trustee before they get close enough to read the stickie.

Our state trustee organization, Community College Association of Texas Trustees (CCATT), now has 16 districts as members and is still growing. Membership dues are based on enrollment numbers and will be used mainly to keep communication flowing with Texas trustees and enhance our colleges' legislative efforts — our mission being:

To unite and mobilize community college trustees to work with the Texas Association of Community Colleges (the state organization for community college presidents) in advocating for and further advancing education, education-related legislation and increased recognition of the impact of community colleges on the economy of Texas.

We have been fighting for a larger part of the small piece of governmental budgets that is not allocated to other causes when we should be showing our legislators how to make the pie (the amount of money in the state budget) bigger by investing in the education our colleges offer. Salaries are determined by education/training, how large salaries are determines what taxes are paid, and what taxes are paid determines the budget. And what part of that budget gets to our colleges determines how educated our workforce will be. As trustees we can and will make a difference and what better investment can our State make.

Kitty Boyle is a trustee from the Dallas
County Community College District in Texas.
She is president of the Community College
Association of Texas Trustees and served as
ACCT Board Chair for the 2007-2008 term.

Texas State Senator Kevin P. Eltife
proudly sporting the "55%/12% stickie"

Effective Advocacy by District and Local Colleges

States, counties, and cities all support community colleges and relationships with their legislative bodies should be attended to and nurtured. Fortunately, the principles of advocacy can be applied generally for the most part, and most of the strategies and tactics commonly used at the national and state levels, with some minor variations, can be used effectively at the local level as well. For community colleges, it is important to remember that "all politics is local."

The task for both the president and board is to make community colleges a part of each legislator's or elected official's thinking, relevant to their agendas, and to connect the college's needs to their needs. To that end, it is important to identify friends of the college within the community and engage them on behalf of the college. These friends may be found among the employers who hire the college's graduates and alumni of the college.

It is essential to effective local-level advocacy to understand how the work of local government is done. While there are many similarities across cities, counties, and towns, certain differences must be mastered. Most governments have Web pages on which they provide information about their agencies, their governing bodies, and how they go about their policy work. Local government Web sites often provide legislative calendars, as well as names and contact information for legislators, committees' chairs and members, and agency heads.

Most, though not all, advocacy work at the local level is concerned with funding, so knowing something about the budget process and who the major players are, such as chairs of appropriations committees, is critical to success.

Lists of committee assignments are available from your local legislature at the beginning of each session. Find out who among your legislators is assigned to committees that handle community college legislation. At the beginning of every legislative session write, e-mail, and call legislators assigned to any committee dealing directly with community colleges and tell them that you are pleased about their assignment and look forward to working with them in support of community colleges.

You should always consult with your college's president and the board of trustees on any advocacy activity you are considering. The work should be done by well-prepared and orchestrated teams of advocates coordinated by the president and involving trustees. A disjointed approach may result in a miscommunication of priorities — or, perhaps worse, may suggest discord among your college leaders.

Knowing when to speak with the appropriate legislators is very important. Trustees should not get ahead of the president or the board when it comes to approaching legislators. It is critical for the board and president to establish priorities and define positions. It's also important to know something about the legislators' positions on community colleges, how they have responded in the past to community college-related legislative action, and who among your board or college leadership would be the best candidate(s) for approaching them.

The president speaks for the college and should attend every public meeting and present the case whenever issues of concern to the college are discussed. Whenever possible, students should be present at those meetings as well and, when appropriate, they should also address the meeting on behalf of the college.

The ideas offered previously on effective written communications, including e-mail, and effective face-to-face meetings at the national and state levels are applicable to the local level as well. Face-to-face interaction is easier at the local level and is the preferred method whenever possible. Invite your local legislators to the campus (again, be sure to invite members of all political parties). During the visits, be sure to provide information about the contributions the college makes to their communities and constituencies. For example, many colleges sponsor an annual legislative breakfast or legislative day on campus. This provides an opportunity to invite all members of local government, state representatives, and their staffs to spend time at the college with the president and trustees. Be sure to prepare materials in advance of legislators' visits that give an overview of your college's contributions to the community and its legislative priorities, as well as contact information for its Legislative Action Team leads.

Remember that legislators are particularly interested in their local colleges. Equally important, as with other elected officials, they must understand the roles and priorities of the community college system before they arrive in the capital for the session. Begin this education process during the election campaign by providing information to the candidates in order to acquaint them with the college, students, and its contributions to the community. For example, show college enrollment in terms of legislative district enrollment and the economic impact of the college on the community. This helps them understand how legislation will affect their districts directly, and it will give you an upper hand when they take office, as they will already be familiar with your identity, goals, and needs.

If possible, sponsor a candidate forum, but be sure to invite all the candidates. Soon after the election, the president and at least one trustee should visit the newly elected legislators for a personal briefing on the college and its value to the community. Written materials, including brochures, fact sheets, and especially information about the economic impact of the college on the community, are helpful in your visits with local legislators. Remember never to leave a legislator's office without leaving paper behind.

KNOW YOUR LEGISLATOR

The first step to establishing effective legislative relations is simply getting to know your local legislators. The more you know, the easier it will be to communicate with them. Part of your job is to familiarize your legislators with community colleges. The most effective methods are letters, e-mails, phone calls, and face-to-face meetings. Encourage your local college and community supporters to call, e-mail, and write, and empower them with your college's legislative priorities, a one-page fact sheet, and talking points. For written correspondence, you may offer your college's supporters a draft letter that they can use as-is or customize. (Note that personal letters are always more effective than form letters, though even form letters are better than nothing, as they show constituents' interest in issues that affect community colleges.) The importance of this steady drumbeat from the legislators' home districts cannot be overestimated. Keep in mind the political proverb, "From phone calls to roll calls, the legislature is a contest of numbers." Remember that steady pressure is arguably the most effective means to effective advocacy for any cause. However, also keep in mind that your legislators are human just like the rest of us, and consider how you would respond to a constant barrage of information from someone eager to tell you about him or herself without ever asking anything about you.

Remember that your goal is a real relationship, which involves two-way communication. Take time to learn about your legislators. Some common sources of information include:

» Legislators' biographies, which include educational background, occupation, and family interests
» People you may both know
» Legislative staff, including aides, research staff, and secretaries (You will find that these people are invaluable gatekeepers to your legislators.)
» Newspapers
» Legislators' own newsletters
» Leadership newsletters
» Statewide community college publications (trustees and presidents associations, state board newsletters, etc.)
» Campaign and political party activities
» Your legislators' Web sites and the ACCT Web site Policy Center at http://www.acct.org/advocacy.

COMMUNICATE WITH YOUR LEGISLATOR ON THE LOCAL LEVEL

Face-to-face personal contact is one of the best ways to meet and understand your legislator. This is also one of the easiest ways to develop access to a legislator. Trustee participation in local fundraisers provides visibility and an opportunity to communicate with your legislator and staff. It also shows your interest in the political process. Legislators rely on local grassroots support. Those who work on a legislator's election campaign are veritably assured of having his or her ear.

» Invite your legislator to a small social gathering with other college officials, their families, or friends — a function where there is no hard sell.
» Invite your legislator to an "orchestrated" gathering sponsored by the college when it is busy; get each candidate on campus for a one-on-one discussion.
» Invite your legislator to speak at graduation.
» Encourage use of college facilities for town meetings and public forums.
» Invite legislative staff to tour the campus, especially when it is busy.
» Never hold a public event without inviting your local public officials.

Write Letters (Paper and Electronic) to Your Legislator

Letters are key to a legislative advocacy campaign in several ways. First, letters allow you to serve as a resource and show how community colleges can better serve the legislator. Not only used by legislators as a source of local information, letters often are "recycled" and quoted to caucuses and on the chamber floors. Second, letters count. Legislators tally up the mail on important issues before the legislature. And third, letters often can be the bearers of good news. People complain about legislators and government all the time, so letters can give them something good to show and tell the folks back home.

Letters written by constituents become the source of a legislator's specialized mailing list. If a legislator votes favorably on a community college request, his or her staff gets a letter out "to inform you that your desired request was acted on favorably." From this correspondence effort, you can establish a relationship with your legislator. When you get a response back, do not stop there — write another letter or e-mail indicating your appreciation.

Steps to an Effective Letter-Writing Campaign

» Send two letters (the first of many to follow during the session) as soon as possible after establishing legislative priorities:
  • An "introductory" letter, signed by the president, to all primary candidates, introducing your college (with a fact sheet), outlining your Legislative Action Team members, and inviting candidates to call for information or to visit the college.
  • After committee assignments, a letter of congratulations, offering to be of service as a resource. "We are pleased with your appointment to (community college-related) Committee; we are pleased that you'll be able to work for community colleges; we pledge our full support."
» Write letters which help legislators keep tabs on constituent success stories on campus. Include student and faculty events, activities, and accomplishments.
» Write letters to the editor. These letters, in response to editorials or observations about specific events, are crucial for keeping community colleges before the eyes of legislators. Every member reads his or her hometown newspaper faithfully. When your letters (or news articles) appear, they add to the steady stream of community college "presence" in the capital.

» Be prepared to write letters throughout the session. When you are contacted by the Legislative Action Team to participate in a letter writing campaign, take the few minutes to write a personal letter based on the basic information the team has given you so that your perspective of the effect on your college will be recorded.

Suggestions for Letter Writers

» Be brief and to the point. Limit your letters to one page.
» Make sure you use your trustee title and/or information describing yourself as a registered voter in the legislator's district.
» Refer to the proposed legislation; i.e., the operating budget, the capital budget, or, if known, the number of a specific bill.
» Explain the effects of the legislation (good or bad).
» Don't attempt to give "expert" opinions; use descriptions based on your local experience and knowledge — which are extremely valid in their own right.
» Request that your legislator take a specific action. Be sure the letter makes clear what you want.
» Direct the letter to the member's capital office during the session.
» Follow up. Send a thank you note if the legislator supports or votes in support of your position. Tell the legislator you have "taken note of his or her position" and have "posted the letter on the college's bulletin board."
» Send a copy of your letter to the Legislative Action Team for its records and/or to craft a response of its own.

Telephone Your Legislator

Obtain phone lists for your legislators at their capital offices. Some states maintain a legislative "hotline," a toll-free 800 number staffed by operators who will direct your message to the appropriate legislator. Don't be embarrassed to call often, but don't be a nuisance; legislators need to hear from you.

Some colleges schedule regular breakfast conference calls with their local legislators that include Chamber of Commerce members and other community members, as well as the college Legislative Action Team.

CAMPUS TOURS: GIVING THE LOCAL FLAVOR TO YOUR EFFORTS

Invite your legislator for a local tour of the college and community. It is important that a tour (1) be structured so the atmosphere is conducive to good communication; and (2) complement an agenda that will provide for discussion of items of importance to your college. As a general rule, tours and meetings with individual legislators are more effective than those involving groups of legislators. Be sure to show specifically how your programs help the state. Highlight not just money items, but also substance and policy.

Before the tours, consider these items:
- What will the tour accomplish for your legislative agenda?
- Will the meeting explain or show how an issue affects the college?
- What will the legislator get out of the tour?
- What is his or her position?

Types of Tours
- Four-on-one briefings, during which a trustee, foundation member, the president, and a community leader brief one legislator
- Class visits
- Facility tours
- Local projects and facilities affiliated with or supported by the college
- Guest speaker
- Breakfast/luncheon visits; arrange transportation to and from the event; have your trustees or foundation pick up the check
- Political awareness days

Planning a Tour

Conduct tours before the legislative session. Avoid tying up legislators' time during elections. Meet with the organizing committee to determine what programs will be visited. Visit good programs that illustrate your point, and ensure that they are in session — legislators like to see and talk to students and instructors. Be sure to take photographs and use wherever possible.

Send a written invitation to the legislator and/or staff.

Plan a simple agenda with specific times. Send a copy to the legislator in advance and stay on schedule. If appropriate and cleared in advance, invite the media and tell the legislator the media will be present. Find out who will be accompanying the legislator. Have board members, advisory committee members, and students participate in the tour and ask some advisory committee members to make brief remarks about their support for programs. Develop a series of success stories about graduates to provide to each legislator and have students tell their own success stories.

Follow the tour with a small private discussion in the president's office. Develop key points you wish to make in conversation: identify exemplary programs, provide data, and outline unmet needs. Pass out one-page fact sheets. Encourage legislative support. Invite the legislator to make brief remarks. Share the remarks with other community college advocacy organizations.

Follow up on the visit by writing a thank you note. Express interest in continuing contact. Consider the visit only one part of an ongoing relationship.

Cautions:
- Don't pile on data that needs interpretation.
- Don't be verbose in written or spoken communications.
- Don't use educational jargon.
- Don't ever "fake" an answer; instead volunteer to retrieve the needed information and report back to the legislator.

Let legislators see and hear and confront everything about their college. Make them feel a part of their college system—and responsible for its well-being. The college is a resource that draws on state dollars, and, as such, it is a concrete example of tax dollars at work.

BE VISIBLE IN THE COMMUNITY

» Attend community activities and local workshops.
» Make community contacts — business, media, civic.
» Increase your involvement in the community beyond things relating only to campus activities.
» Build linkages with other organizations; encourage groups such as the League of Women Voters to hold candidate forums on campus.
» Attend meetings, breakfasts, or lunches sponsored periodically by legislators. Ask to be notified.

Meeting with Your Legislators

Ideas on preparing for, conducting, and following up on meetings offered for the national and state levels are also appropriate at the local level. Your action plan should include a schedule for letter and e-mail contacts, phone calls, and visits.

Face-to-face meetings are still the best way to communicate the community college message to state and local legislators. With good planning and preparation, these meetings can be highly productive. There are some basic guidelines to keep in mind when planning a visit with local legislators and elected officials:
- Schedule your appointment well in advance.
- It may be easier to obtain an appointment for a group.
- Prepare for the visit by becoming familiar with the legislation or issue you will discuss in your meeting.
- Take along a business leader who is an expert on the issue. If possible, also bring a student or two.
- If you plan to visit more than one legislator, allow sufficient time to allow for possible delays and to permit you to get to the next appointment on time.
- Be on time and willing to wait. If your appointment is delayed, use the time to get to know the staffer.

- Pick a spokesperson in advance.
- Be clear about what you want.
- Keep it simple. Plan your presentation.
- Thank him or her for past support for the community college agenda.
- Be prepared to answer questions.
- Listen carefully.

After the visits, the committee should debrief on what worked and didn't work. If so indicated by your debriefing, modify your Action Team and strategy. Publicly and privately thank the legislators who support community colleges. Stay in touch during the off-season. As with any relationship, contacts with legislators must be nurtured in order for them to function smoothly over the long run.

The goal is to develop a respectful and supportive relationship. Be mindful of potential pitfalls. For example, some officials could see the college as a potential place for patronage, a way to influence the awarding of contracts to vendors, etc. Don't cross the line or encourage the expectation of favors that could compromise the integrity of the board and college. Remember you are always advocating on behalf of students and the greater good, not special interests.

PERSONAL PERSPECTIVE
Ten Ways to be an Effective Advocate for Your College and Its Students

By Wayne Newton

1) First and foremost, the board of trustees and each of its members should develop a sound process and relationship that generates a productive work environment. The board should always put the best face on the institution. The stakeholders need to see a professionally governed operation at all times. If the board's operation is always focused on student needs and effective stewardship, the public will more willingly support the financial needs of the college.

2) Be intimately familiar with numerous student success stories and commit them to memory so you can share them with both supporters and critics. Set the best of examples in all of your dealings. Remember that you are under the watchful eye of your stakeholders both on and off the campus.

3) With the image of the college enhanced through positive outcomes, legislators will take note and be more willing to support the financial needs of the college. Be sure the college facilities are open to them. Invite legislators as graduation speakers. The civic benefits to your students and community far outweigh any political risks that might creep into these events.

4) Use every public occasion to promote the advantages of the college and its people. Your attitude as a trustee carries an enormous influence on how the public learns about and views the college.

5) Be sure that your representatives know the importance of their support for public education. Don't assume that the legislators that you support know of your service on the college's board, or that they will naturally support the college without your encouragement.

6) Acquaint yourself with the financial trends that adversely affect your students' education expenses. Relate the numbers in appropriations bills to real people.

7) Do not operate as a solo institution. By working in concert with other advocates including, if applicable, your state system, to improve the system's financial support, you will secure greater support for community colleges overall and thereby increase support for your own college. Working as a system may take more time, but in the long run it will be much more productive than working in a silo.

8) Know the return on the public investment in your college. View your budget as an investment in the future of your community, and share this view with legislators and the public, including your student body.
9) Avoid being a single-interest trustee. Provide the vision needed to anticipate future programs and the changes needed to meet those objectives.
10) When the action items above are accomplished, the college will naturally attract a highly qualified staff and students will have a positive experience. These satisfied students and staff will serve as the best marketers by telling their friends, family, and others about your learning environment.

Conclusion

The work of advocacy is never done. It is a permanent item on every college's agenda. And it requires persistence, steady pressure, and constant feedback, not to mention countless letters, e-mails, phone calls, and visits from many different supporters. One hundred contacts by 100 different individuals are worth more than the same hundred contacts by one or a few individuals. Maintaining a steady contact with legislators is important year-round — not only when you want the legislators' help. Reinforcing and supporting the unique role of the president, your "quarterback" when it comes to advocacy, is crucial. Board and president planning and establishing legislative priorities will ensure that you focus your energy and efforts on the most important needs of students, the college, and the community. It is important that the college community be aware of the commitment made by the board and individual trustees on their behalf. The reward for the board and the president translates to respect and admiration from students, faculty, and staff. The college knows when trustees and the presidents are advocating on behalf of the greater good of the college and the community.

Wayne T. Newton has served as an ACCT Retreat Services facilitator for nearly 200 community colleges throughout the country. He has served as a trustee of Kirkwood (IA) Community College for 30 years and served as Chairman of the Board of Trustees nearly twenty. He has also held all of the executive offices of ACCT including the Presidency in 1984-85. He has been a delegate to and President of the Iowa Association of Community College Trustees.

PERSONAL PERSPECTIVE
Advocacy for the Community College CEO: Working with the Board Team

By George Boggs

At no other time in their history have community colleges received the degree of recognition from the public and policymakers for the work that they do. This recognition is the result of many years of sustained advocacy by state and national community college organizations and — most importantly — by community college leaders and trustees who are the members of these associations. Although recognition is important, financial support to serve students and communities is even more important. Just as in the shaping of the community college image, CEOs and trustees are key spokespersons and advocates for their institutions in the competition for limited public funds. The most important advocacy for funding support must be planned and coordinated as it is directed toward policymakers at the local, state, and federal levels.

CEOs who regularly brief their trustees on legislative issues are a step ahead when concerted effort is called for. In addition, for CEOs to be most successful in their advocacy efforts, they should utilize the political expertise on their boards. Boards and CEOs also need to be vigilant in watching and responding to the efforts of special interest groups that propose legislation that could hurt the college or its students.

Legislative advocacy does not begin when there is a need to lobby for or against a bill. Instead, it is necessary to develop a relationship with legislators and their staffs over a period of time. CEOs should work with their boards to develop a legislative and communications advocacy plan so that all parties know their responsibilities and where to get needed information. Board members who are either publicly elected or politically appointed often have an advantage in gaining access to legislators. It is also important for legislators to see the college CEO and the board members as leaders who can sway public opinion. That means the CEO and board members must be visible in the community, and they must support community activities and attend community events. Writing opinion pieces for the editorial pages of local newspapers or participating in radio or television interviews on public policy issues are other ways that CEOs and trustees can gain an image as influential advocates. CEOs can provide essential assistance to trustees who take up the challenge to write an article or an opinion editorial or participate in a radio or television interview.

Information on education can be provided to political candidates to help them build their campaign platforms. CEOs or trustees can also act to moderate candidate debates or forums. This kind of support and visibility often makes a difference in gaining access to busy legislators after the election. CEOs, however, should be cautious about publicly endorsing one political candidate over others, especially if the office is one that will influence the distribution of resources to the college or the appointment of college trustees.

Legislators and their staff members should be invited to campus as often as possible to learn about the college, its programs, and its needs. They can be given a short tour and an opportunity to visit and take photographs with students and faculty members. CEOs should make sure that legislators and their staff members see the areas that need improvement and not just the modern facilities and programs that everyone at the college is proud of. The involvement of trustees in these tours is an important way for them to be involved in advocacy and to know the needs of their campuses.

In some instances, it will be necessary to mobilize the college community and its supporters to advocate for needed legislation. Trustees, foundation board members, and college advisory committee members can be very helpful by calling the legislators they know and by sending advocacy letters on their business letterhead. The CEO can improve the response rate of these college supporters by enclosing a sample letter and talking points with the request for assistance. State and national community college advocacy organizations are important sources of information about proposed legislation and its effect on community colleges.

CEOs should take the lead both in communicating frequently with legislators at the local, state, and federal levels and in keeping the board members aware of important legislative issues. CEOs should also encourage trustees to build upon their political connections as appointed or elected officials to advocate with state and federal policymakers. Communications with legislators should appeal to any interests these policymakers might have that are related to the college mission. When writing letters to legislators, CEOs should be sure that all board members receive copies. Similarly, when a trustee sends advocacy letters, the CEO and all other board members should receive copies. When legislators respond positively, they should receive thank you notes from the CEO, and the support should be noted at board meetings. The community college CEO and board are the most effective advocacy team for their colleges if they act together in a planned and coordinated way.

George R. Boggs is president and chief executive officer
of the American Association of Community Colleges (AACC).

APPENDIX A

GLOSSARY OF CONGRESSIONAL TERMS

Act
Term for legislation that has passed both houses of Congress, signed by the President, or passed over his veto, thus becoming law.

Amendment
A Congress Member's proposal to change the language or content in a bill or act.

Bill
Legislative proposal originating in either house of Congress. Bills are numbered by either H.R. (for bills originating in the House) or S. (for bills originating in the Senate).

Cloture
Closing off debate. The Senate put an end to unlimited debate in 1917 when it provided that two-thirds of those present may invoke the "rule of cloture" and set a time limit for discussion. In 1975, support necessary for cloture was changed to three-fifths of the entire Senate; in 1979, a 100-hour cap on debate was imposed after cloture was invoked to limit the use of delaying amendments.

Committee
A legislative sub-organization in the that handles a duty more specific than the general duties of Congress. Through committee participation, Congress Members become intimately familiar with specialized knowledge of committee-related matters. Committees observe ongoing legislative processes, identify matters for review, research and analyze information, and recommend legislative action.

Committee of the Whole
A different set of legislative rules applies when the House resolves itself into "The Committee of the Whole House on the State of the Union." For example, when a bill is

reported out of committee, it goes to the Rules Committee where procedural specifications on how the bill will be considered on the floor are designed. The bill and the rule on the bill then go to the floor of the House for consideration and a rule must be approved first. After the rule passes, the Speaker of the House declares that the "House is resolved into the Committee on the Whole House on the State of the Union," and leaves the chair after appointing a Chairman to preside.

In the Committee on the Whole there are special expediting rules:
- A quorum is 100 Members.
- A motion to close debate is in order by unanimous consent, or the majority of the Members present.
- The five-minute rule is in effect for debate on amendments.
- All bills, motions, or propositions involving a tax, appropriations of money or property, releasing liability to the United States for money or property, or referring any claim to the Court of Claims, must be first considered in a Committee of the Whole.

The order of business under the Committee of the Whole is as follows: debate on the bill, debate on the amendments, votes on the amendments. The Committee then rises and the Speaker returns to the chair and announces: "under the rule, the previous question is ordered." This means that no further debate is allowed. Each amendment that was successful in the Committee of the Whole is now offered and voted on. Then the bill as amended is voted on.

Conference Committee
A temporary panel of House and Senate negotiators charged with resolving differences between similar House and Senate bills.

Congressional Record
The daily printed account of the proceedings of both Senate and House chambers, with debate, statements, etc. reported verbatim.

Executive Session
A meeting closed to the public.

Filibuster
Senate device used to delay or prevent a vote by time-consuming talk. This tactic is often used by a minority of members in an effort to prevent a vote on a bill that would probably pass if brought to a vote. Can only be stopped by the Senate invoking cloture.

Germaneness
House rules require that amendments to a bill relate to the subject matter under consideration, that they must be germane. Any Member may raise a point of order that an

amendment is non-germane and should be ruled out of order. However, the Speaker has considerable discretion in ruling on points of order involving germaneness. Deciding which amendments are or are not to be considered gives the Speaker a powerful tool to shape legislation. The House, by majority vote, often accepts the recommendation of its Rules Committee that specified non-germane amendments are permitted. This gives the Rules Committee, controlled by the majority leadership, considerable power to push its legislative agenda. In the Senate, the majority party has far less power to control the legislative agenda. Amendments do not have to be germane unless they are offered to a general appropriations bill. Even then, the Senate can decide to accept them as germane by a simple majority vote. All amendments offered after cloture has been invoked, however, must be germane.

Joint Committee
Committee composed of a specific number of members of both the House and the Senate.

Majority Leader
The leader of the majority party in the Senate is called the Majority Leader. The Majority Leader in the House is second in command of the majority party, after the Speaker.

Mark Up
Subcommittee or committee work session scheduled after hearings at which the subcommittee or committee goes through a measure, section by section — revising language, penciling in new phrases, adding amendments, combining two or more bills into one vehicle, etc.

Minority Leader
Leader of the minority party in the House or Senate.

Quorum
A majority of Members duly chosen and sworn, 218 in the House and 51 in the Senate (in the absence of deaths or resignations). A quorum is necessary to conduct business. Senator especially while sitting in the Committee of the Whole. The presiding officer often controls quorum calls, using the delay to further his legislative goals. s may object to the absence of a quorum at almost any time, which makes quorum roll calls an integral part of Senate parliamentary tactics. House rules are more restrictive,

Ranking Minority Member
The most senior minority party member on a committee.

Recess
Concludes the legislative day, with a set time for reconvening, usually more than three days after adjournment.

Report

A printed record of a committee's actions and views on a particular bill or matter.

Rider

A provision, usually not related, tacked on to a bill that its sponsor hopes to get through more easily by including in other legislation.

Session

Each Congress is composed of two annual sessions. A new session of Congress begins each January 3 at noon and continues until adjourned "sine die."

Sine Die

Adjournment without definitely fixing a day for reconvening; Adjournment Sine Die is literally, "adjournment without a day." This term is usually used to connote the final adjournment of a session of Congress.

Speaker of the House

Presiding officer of the House, leader of the majority party in the House (although there is no constitutional requirement that the Speaker be a Representative), and next in line to the Vice-President for succession to the Presidency. The Speaker is one of the most powerful offices in Washington.

Suspension of the Rules

An expedited procedure for considering legislation in the House. Debate is severely restricted and amendments are not allowed, but a two-thirds majority is required for passage.

Tabling Motion

A proposal to remove a bill from immediate consideration. It is often used to kill a measure.

Unanimous Consent

Almost any rule in the House and Senate can be overlooked by unanimous consent. The Senate relies on unanimous consent agreements to define legislative ground rules for particular measures, which protects the rights of the minority party and forces Members to work with one another. The House uses unanimous consent agreements relatively sparingly — usually to adopt a non-controversial measure and legislative ground rules are set by majority, often party line, vote.

APPENDIX B

CONGRESSIONAL COMMITTEES

There are five basic types of Congressional Committees:

- **Authorizing Committees:** Also called legislative committees, these committees write new legislation, amend existing legislation, reauthorize programs, and conduct oversight hearings to determine if the government is carrying out the laws in conformance with Congressional intent.
- **Budget Committees:** Budget committees are responsible for setting annual spending targets for the government in broad categories, such as defense, transportation, and Social Security. The budget function category that relates to education expenditures comes under the broad classification of Labor, Health and Human Services, Education and Related Agencies and is numbered "Function 500." The spending targets set by the Budget Committees may not be exceeded in the appropriations process.
- **Appropriations Committees:** These are the committees that approve the actual spending for programs by appropriating funds from the federal treasury for each federal program, responsibility, or government activity. The House and Senate Appropriations Committees each have 13 separate Subcommittees, drafting 13 separate appropriations measures each year.
- **Tax Committees:** These revenue-raising committees have jurisdiction over the tax code, social security, and unemployment insurance. They specify how revenue will be raised through taxes and fees, and decide which tax credits, deductions, and income exemptions will be maintained in the tax code. The House committee is called the Committee on Ways and Means; the Senate committee is the Committee on Finance.
- **Select and Special Committees:** These committees are created by Congress to study special problems or concerns. They hold hearings, conduct investigations or studies, and issue reports. Usually they do not draft legislation, and they usually last through only one or two Congresses.

APPENDIX C

THE FEDERAL BUDGET PROCESS

The federal government operates on a fiscal year that begins October 1 and ends the following September 30. As required by law, the President triggers the annual budget process each year by submitting a proposed budget to Congress in early February. The President's proposed budget outlines administration priorities through its spending requests for federal agencies and programs, and it includes projections of revenues, projections on economic growth rates and inflation rates, deficit levels, and proposals for raising additional revenues.

Once the President's budget is received on Capitol Hill, the Congressional Budget Office prepares a report (usually by mid-February) for House and Senate Budget Committees that analyzes the President's budget. House and Senate Budget Committees notify authorizing committees to transmit their views and estimates on funding needed for programs back to them by a specified target date (usually six weeks after Congress receives the President's budget). The Budget Committees then hold hearings and draft separate budget resolutions, which eventually will be passed in the same form by both Houses. The Congressional Budget is a "concurrent resolution" (passed by both Houses and enforced by rules of each body, but not signed by the President) used as blueprint to guide the appropriations and revenue decision-making process.

Until the budget resolution is adopted, as a general rule, Congress is prohibited by the Congressional Budget Act from considering any revenue, spending, entitlement, debt, or credit legislation. This prohibition is enforced through the parliamentary process of points of order raised against consideration of such legislation until a jointly approved resolution is adopted. The Congressional Budget Act specifies that a budget resolution — basically a "spending plan" — be adopted by April 15. Congress frequently misses this target date. House rules permit the House Appropriations Committee to move bills even if a jointly approved budget resolution is not in place.

Once a jointly approved budget resolution is adopted, the House and Senate Appropriations Committees meet and decide how to divide up the pie of available dollars for spending among the 13 Appropriations Subcommittees. This "parceling out" of available dollars by the full Appropriations Committee to the 13 Subcommittees is referred to as the "602(b) allocation process." Education and job training programs are funded by the Labor, Health and Human Services, Education and Related Agencies (LHHS-ED) Subcommittee of the Appropriations Committee. Both the Senate and House LHHS-ED Appropriations Subcommittee draft separate appropriations measures, which must (like all other legislation) be approved by the originating chamber, then set to conference to resolve differences, passed in the same form by both chambers, and finally signed by the President before they become law.

House rules require all appropriations bills to be completed by June 30 (this deadline is frequently missed). Senate rules require completion of appropriation measures by September 30 (the last day of the fiscal year). If all 13 spending bills are not completed and signed by October 1, Congress must pass a temporary or stopgap spending measure known as a continuing resolution to allow federal agencies to continue to operate (pay salaries, etc.) until the appropriations bills are enacted. Upon enactment, funds are made available to federal departments and agencies to fund programs under their jurisdiction.

APPENDIX D

ADVOCACY RESOURCES & LINKS

Note: Clickable links to all of the resources below and more are available on the ACCT Web site at www.acct.org/advocacy/links.

The Association of Community College Trustees Web Site
www.acct.org
ACCT's Web site is the first stop online for advocacy and other resources tailored specifically for community college trustees. Go to www.acct.org/advocacy for ACCT's Latest Action in Washington (LAW) alerts, which detail pressing legislative actions as they happen, as well as information on the Congressional Community College Caucuses, community college legislative priorities, federal education funding by program, ACCT letters to U.S. Congress, successful advocacy toolkits, National Legislative Summit materials, as well as an interactive Policy Center and useful resource links, including all of those listed below.

The American Association of Community Colleges Web Site
www.aacc.nche.edu/Advocacy/
The AACC Web site's advocacy page features advocacy news, resources, federal register, lists of key committees and subcommittees, testimony, and more.

ACCT Policy Center/CongressWeb
www.congressweb.com/cweb4/index.cfm?orgcode=acct
This Web page makes it easy to locate and contact your federal representatives.

The White House
www.whitehouse.gov
This Web site connects you to all federal Web sites. Visitors can also view White House daily briefings and Administration priorities.

U.S. Senate

www.senate.gov

This Web site allows you to look up information on Senators, committees, legislative activities, floor action and more.

- Committee on Health, Education, Labor, and Pensions: help.senate.gov
- Subcommittee on Education and Early Childhood Development: help.senate. gov/Education_sub_index.html
- Committee on Appropriations: appropriations.senate.gov
- Subcommittee on Labor, Health and Human Services, Education, and Related Agencies: appropriations.senate.gov/labor.cfm
- Budget Committee: budget.senate.gov

U.S. House of Representatives

www.house.gov

This Web site connects you to information on Members of Congress, committees, floor action and more. It gives you directions on how to write your Representative, a tour of the Capitol and provides links to other parts of government.

- Committee on Education and Labor: edlabor.house.gov/index.shtml
- Subcommittee on Higher Education, Lifelong Learning, and Competitiveness: edlabor.house.gov/hearings/higher-education
- Committee on Appropriations: appropriations.house.gov
- Subcommittee on Labor, Health and Human Services, Education, and Related Agencies: appropriations.house.gov/Subcommittees/sub_lhhse.shtml
- Budget Committee: budget.house.gov

U.S. Congress on the Internet

thomas.loc.gov

Managed by the Library of Congress, this Web site provides information on legislation being considered in Congress. It includes bill text, bill status information, the Congressional Record, committee reports and more.

U.S. Department of Education

www.ed.gov

Information on the Department's initiatives, education programs and services, and publications. It has a special section on student financial assistance, helpful to students planning for postsecondary education.

U.S. Department of Labor

www.dol.gov

Information on welfare to work, minimum wage, small business and other labor and workforce issues. There is a special section on the Secretary's priorities.

Office of the Community College Liaison
www.ed.gov/about/offices/list/ovae/pi/cclo/index.html
Information specific to community colleges and is housed within the Office of Vocational and Adult Education, U.S. Department of Education.

National Science Foundation
www.nsf.gov
Information on the independent agency's mission, programs, and grants available to educational institutions. Look here for the latest on the Advanced Technology Education program.

Government Accountability Office
www.gao.gov
The Government Accountability Office (GAO) is an agency that works for Congress and the American people. Congress asks GAO to study the programs and expenditures of the federal government. GAO, commonly called the investigative arm of Congress or the congressional watchdog, is independent and nonpartisan.

Office of the Federal Register
www.gpoaccess.gov
The Federal Register is the official daily publication for rules, proposed rules, and notices of Federal agencies and organizations, as well as executive orders and other presidential documents.

Committee for Education Funding
www.cef.org
The Committee for Education Funding (CEF) is comprised of over 90 organizations dedicated to the goal of achieving adequate federal financial support for the nation's educational system. ACCT is a member of CEF. This site provides information on the funding of federal education programs.

How Our Laws are Made is a publication of the House Rules Committee. This is an excellent small booklet which describes the legislative process. You may request a free copy from your Representative or you can read or download the full publication at thomas.loc. gov/home/lawsmade.toc.html.

Education Budget Alert
Education Budget Alert, an annual compilation of federal education programs, analyzed and compared for impact, with the funding levels proposed by the President's Budget. This publication is prepared by the Committee for Education Funding (CEF). For more information, call CEF at 202-383-0097, or write to The Committee for Education Funding, 122 C Street, NW, Ste. 280, Washington, DC 20001. www.cef.org

Roll Call
Roll Call is the daily newspaper for Congress. Since 1955, Roll Call's mission has been to deliver superior coverage of the people, politics, process and policy on Capitol Hill. www.rollcall.com

Your State, City, and County Web Sites
Your state, city, and county Web sites. Many of these provide information on how their legislative process works; names and contact information for legislators and committee members and chair; legislative and budget process calendars, and more.

Your State Community College Association Web Site and Public Policy Staffs
Links to the majority of state community college associations are available at http://www.acct.org/resources/links/college-associations.php. If you do not see your state's association listed on this page, please contact ACCT at acctinfo@acct.org.

APPENDIX E

KEY TERMS AND DEFINITIONS

Carl D. Perkins Career and Technical Education Act: Perkins Act programs are intended to enhance educational opportunities for all career and technical education students at public secondary and postsecondary schools. Funds are disseminated to states, which in turn allocate funds by formula to secondary and postsecondary schools. State funds are used to provide technical expertise and professional development opportunities to teachers and administrators, develop accountability systems, and support student organizations. Funds that are directed to public secondary and community-based postsecondary schools are used for program improvement, including equipment, curriculum development, and professional development.

Community-Based Job Training Grants (CBJTG): The Community-Based Job Training Grants (CBJTG) program funds help strengthen the role of community colleges in promoting the U.S. workforce's full potential. The grants are employer-focused and build on the President's High Growth Job Training Initiative, a national model for demand-driven workforce development implemented by strategic partnerships between the workforce investment system, employers, and community colleges and other training providers. The primary purpose of the CBJTG program is to build the capacity of community colleges to train workers to develop the skills required to succeed in high growth/high demand industries.

Federal Family Education Loan (FFELP) and Direct Loan (DL) Programs: The FFELP and DL programs help make low-interest, variable rate loans available to students and their families to pay for the costs of attending postsecondary institutions. Direct loans are loans provided and serviced directly through the federal government. FFELP leverages private capital from banks and other lenders, and are administered primarily through private companies and state and non-profit agencies. Federal loan programs assist a broad spectrum of students and their parents. The federal government pays loan interest for students with demonstrated need while they are in school and during grace and deferment periods. Eligible undergraduate students can borrow up to $23,500 to pursue their studies.

Federal Supplemental Educational Opportunity Grants (FSEOG): The FSEOG program provides an additional source of grant aid for exceptionally needy students. Supplemental Grant recipients use these funds in combination with other forms of grant, loan, and work-study aid to meet their total expenses. Any academically qualified student may apply for aid to complete a certificate of degree program. First priority for Supplemental Grant awards are Pell Grant recipients. The federal share of the award under the program cannot exceed 75 percent; the remaining 25 percent of the award must be contributed by the participating institution. The maximum annual award is $4,000; the minimum is $100.

Leveraging Educational Assistance Partnerships (LEAP): Through matching formula grants to states, the LEAP Program provides grant aid to students with substantial financial need to help them pay for their postsecondary education costs. This partnership between states and the federal government requires that states match federal LEAP funding. When the amount of federal funding reaches $30 million, states that wish to participate must match the allocation 2 to 1.

Pell Grant: A federal Pell Grant, unlike a loan, does not have to be repaid. Pell Grants are awarded only to undergraduate students who have not earned a bachelor's or professional degree. (A professional degree would include a degree in a field such as pharmacy or dentistry.) For many students, Pell Grants provide a foundation of financial aid to which other aid may be added. To determine eligibility for a Pell Grant, the U.S. Department of Education uses a formula established by Congress. This formula evaluates financial information a student supplies, the cost of attendance at their institution, full or part-time status, and whether the student attends for a full academic year or less. Pell Grant funds, and the maximum grant, are appropriated annually by Congress. The maximum award for the current academic year (2009-10) is $5,350. More than 2 million community college students receive Pell Grants annually.

Perkins Loans: The Federal Perkins Loan Program provides low-interest loans to needy students. Loan capital is procured from federal appropriations, institutions' contributions, and from collections from prior borrowers. Funds are allocated by formula to institutions for distribution to eligible students. Eligible undergraduate students may borrow up to $5,500 annually, with a maximum aggregate undergraduate limit of $27,500 (as of the 2009-10 academic year).

Strengthening Institutions and Hispanic-Serving Institutions Grants: These programs award competitive grants to accredited institutions that offer undergraduate degrees. For Strengthening Institution grants, institutions must have relatively limited resources and serve a high percentage of needy students. For Hispanic-Serving Institutions grants, at least 25 percent of the full-time undergraduates must qualify as Hispanic enrollment and 50 percent or more classified as low-income students.

TRIO: TRIO is a compilation of five programs that provide direct outreach and student support services to high school, college, and university students. The programs are designed to encourage individuals from disadvantaged backgrounds to enter and complete college. By law, at least two-thirds of the students served by TRIO programs must be the first in their family to attend college.

Work-Study: The federal Work-Study program leverages resources from schools and the private sector to provide opportunities for students to earn money to pay for college. The program is also designed to encourage students receiving federal financial aid to participate in community service. In addition to providing self-help assistance for students, federal Work-Study funds help create partnerships between the federal government, postsecondary schools, students, and communities.

APPENDIX F

KNOW YOUR LEGISLATOR

Please use this form in building the groundwork for a successful meeting on Capitol Hill during the NLS with your Senator(s) and/or Representative(s)! Please fill out a form for each member of the Congressional delegation.

Your Representative/Senator: _____

Congressional District: _____ State: _____

Washington, DC Office Information

Office Address: _____

Phone Number: _____Fax Number: _____

Scheduler: _____

Committee Assignments: _____

_____

_____

Member of the Community College Caucus? _____

Legislative Assistants for:

Education:_____

Job Training: _____

Budget/Appropriations: _____

Tax: _____

Legislator's Priorities: _____

District Office Information

Office Address: _____

_____

Phone Number: _____   Fax Number: _____

Scheduler: _____

District Representative: _____

Community College Background

Has your Representative/Senator visited your campus?

_____

_____

_____

Is your Representative/Senator active in your community college activities?

_____

_____

_____

Did your Representative/Senator attend a community college?

_____

_____

_____

Teach at a community college?

_____

_____

_____

APPENDIX G

SUCCESSFUL MEETING TIPS

» **Be on time, flexible, friendly and brief:** Arrive early and be willing to wait. Delayed appointments can be very beneficial if they give you time to get to know the Member's staff. Meeting with staff can be as productive as seeing the Member personally. Flexibility is important because Members' schedules get juggled at a moment's notice. Stick to the issues and facts, and don't outstay your welcome. Congressional offices are friendly places and are open to meeting with visitors from the state or district they represent.

» **Ask about your member's priorities:** As with any good relationship, it is important to have give and take. So ask your member what his or her priorities are — it is an excellent opportunity to find out more about them and their agenda. It also can be an opportunity to work together on additional issues.

» **Ask for support:** Your Representative, Senator, or their staff should be able to give you an indication of the member's level of support for the community college priorities. It is appropriate for you to ask their position.

» **ACCT and AACC:** Remind members and staff that the two national associations representing community college trustees and CEOs (ACCT and AACC) are headquartered in Washington, D.C. and are available and always willing to provide information on community college issues.

» **Photo Op:** Ask to take a photograph with your legislator so that the public information officer at your college can send a news release and picture to your local newspaper for publicity. This helps communicate to your community that you are actively working on their behalf.

» **Get Business Cards:** Ask for business cards of any staff members you talk to for easy reference when writing your thank you letter. Remember to leave your business card or college information when you are visiting their office.

Board Leadership Services
www.acct.org/services
From the Association of Community College Trustees

ACCT Center for Effective Governance
www.acct.org/resources/center

President/CEO Searches
www.acct.org/services/searches

Board Retreats and Workshops
www.acct.org/services/retreats

College President Evaluations
www.acct.org/services/evaluation

Board Self-Assessments
www.acct.org/services/assessment

Interim President Placements
www.acct.org/services/interim

Mediation & Conflict Resolution
www.acct.org/services/conflict

For more information about ACCT Board Leadership Services, contact:
Dr. Narcisa A. Polonio
Vice President for Research, Education, and Board Leadership Services

Tel: 202.775.4670 • Cell: 202.276.1983 • E-mail: npolonio@acct.org • Fax: 202.223.1297
Association of Community College Trustees
1233 20th Street, NW, Suite 301 • Washington, DC 20036

ACCT PUBLICATIONS

www.acct.org/resources/publications

Trustee Quarterly

The official quarterly magazine of the Association of Community College Trustees, designed to keep readers up to date on current events and best practices relating to board governance and the community college sector. TQ regularly covers such topics as public policy, governance, advocacy, leadership, CEO hiring and relations, ethics, finance, fundraising, legal issues and technology. The magazine is a complimentary service to ACCT members and is available for subscription.

The Trustee's Role in Effective Advocacy: Engaging Citizen Action to Advance Educational Opportunities in Your Community

by the Association of Community College Trustees (2009).

This publication details everything trustees need to know about exercising their voices and influence on behalf of community colleges at the local, state, regional and federal levels, including practical "how-to" information, case studies from community college leaders, and useful forms and other resource information.

The Trustee's Role in Fundraising: From Arm's Length to Knee Deep

by Philip M. Ringle, Ph.D. (2008).

This monograph details the increasing importance of fundraising to maintaining and growing community colleges. Dr. Ringle explains what trustees need to know about institutional advancement, including the limitations of traditional funding sources, what board members can do as individuals and as a cohesive board, the components of development and more. A provocative case study by ACCT Vice President Narcisa A. Polonio, Ed.D. is included to help trustees and presidents learn to maneuver the waters before diving into a capital campaign.

The Board Chair: A Guide for Leading Community College Boards

edited by Vaughn A. Sherman and Cindra J. Smith (2002).

The board chair plays a crucial leadership role at a community college. What are the key traits needed by the chair? What are the chair's roles and responsibilities? How should a chair organize and run a meeting? What sort of relationship does the chair need to have with the CEO? These and other important questions are answered by this handbook, written by former board chairs.

Trusteeship in Community Colleges: A Guide to Effective Governance

by Cindra J. Smith (2000).

This 220-page guide for effective governance explains the unique role of community college governing boards and the many variations in how trustees are chosen and how boards govern.

Community College Trustees: Leading on Behalf of their Communities
by George B. Vaughan and Iris M. Weisman (1997).

 Turn to this book for the answers — many of them unexpected — to questions such as: Who are the members of community college governing boards? How are trustees different and how are they similar? How do trustees view the responsibility of governing a community college? What are the rewards that motivate them to continue serving? What characteristics would board members expect in an ideal president? What do presidents think of the boards for whom they work? What do presidents look for in an idea board? How do trustees and presidents grade their relationships? These questions and many, many more are answered in this staple text.

Visit **www.acct.org/resources/publications** for the most current list of available publications and information on how to order copies.